Wonder, Love, and Praise

A Supplement to The Hymnal 1982

Church Publishing Incorporated, New York

10 9

Preface

*Resolved, . . . that the Standing Commission on Church Music be
directed to continue preparing supplements to* The Hymnal 1982 *which
provide this Church with additional service music, inclusive language
hymnody, additional texts in languages other than English, including
texts printed in more than one language, additional hymnody related to
the lectionary and rites of the Book of Common Prayer, and texts and
tunes written since the compiling of the present Hymnal.*

This resolution was passed at the seventy-first General Convention in 1994 and
led to the creation of *Wonder, Love, and Praise: A Supplement to The Hymnal
1982*. This supplement fulfills the mandate of the resolution. It should be seen as
a continuation of the current hymnal—to be used in conjunction with it. The
numbering begins with the next consecutive number (721) after the last hymn in
The Hymnal 1982. This supplement is also part of a continuing process of
liturgical and musical enrichment and augmentation which offer an expanding
vocabulary of spoken and sung prayer. The church has entered a new frontier of
inclusive hospitality, not only in welcoming all to the table, but also in providing
rites, forms, and music which encourage the sharing of one's cultural story to
foster the unity proclaimed in the gospel. This supplement honors that pilgrim-
age and affirms "the participation of all in the Body of Christ the Church, while
recognizing our diverse natures as children of God." (Preface, *The Hymnal
1982*).

As the Standing Commission on Church Music began to work, we soon realized
that there were factors which were making our job difficult: changing musical
styles and tastes, evolving visions of mission, and rapidly expanding communi-
cations and technology. These factors made the development of clear objectives
elusive. Gradually we developed general guidelines that served us well and
enabled a clearer vision to come, ultimately, into focus. First, we wanted to
prepare a resource that adds to *The Hymnal 1982*. Second, we sought to embody
a musical simplicity that encourages immediate participation. Third, we wanted
to offer a breadth of musical styles from many cultures.

The church's music is changing significantly as we approach the twenty-first
century. This reality often dictated that we make decisions about the contents of
this book that some may find unusual for the Episcopal Church. We also felt
strongly that within the charge we had been given was the opportunity to offer a
musical table laden with a variety of spiritual food—from appetizer to dessert.
We have left the decision about what makes up a well-balanced meal to those
who come to the feast.

As an eclectic collection of hymns and spiritual songs, this supplement provides a diversity that will be readily useable at local, diocesan, provincial and national occasions which require broad cultural resources. Many of the songs found here have already made their way into the repertoire of Episcopal parishes searching for music appropriate to their own context. Much of it has proved accessible to parishes both small and large, with multiple expressions of corporate worship, and to rural, suburban, and urban communities.

Recognizing the lack of public occasions in our society which foster singing, we also looked for music that would encourage informal participation. We expect that much of this music will be assimilated into parish life apart from corporate worship, whether at retreats, parish suppers, prayer services, or at home. Finally, we believe that *Wonder, Love, and Praise* will help the baptized and baptizing community manifest a respect for the dignity of every person through its sung prayer by embodying the vision of Christ to love and to serve.

The title, *Wonder, Love, and Praise,* is taken from the final phrase of the Charles Wesley text "Love divine, all loves excelling." By choosing these words we hoped to convey our desire to leave behind the current debates about taste and style, go beyond expressions of musical unity, and affirm the need of every Christian to praise God in song.

We wish to acknowledge the wise counsel of Clayton L. Morris, Liturgical Officer of the Episcopal Church, and the excellent work of William Wunsch, editor.

The Standing Commission on Church Music, 1994-1997
Owen Burdick
Carol Doran
Marilyn Haskel, Chair
Carl Haywood
John Hooker, Vice-Chair
Gethin Hughes
Henry Louttit
Mark MacDonald
Bernardo Murray
Nancy Newman
Catherine Nichols
Sue Reid

Publisher's Note

Wonder, Love, and Praise: *A Supplement to The Hymnal 1982* was designed for accessibility and easy use. The first line of the hymn or spiritual song appears at the top of each selection, a practice common to most hymnals today. Service music selections use all the titles common to The Book of Common Prayer and *The Hymnal 1982*. There is an index for the service music which lists first lines as well as all the titles, for ease of location.

The typeface chosen is clear and large on a page that is free of distracting technical markings. Accompaniments have been included in this volume so that they are readily available. As in *The Hymnal 1982* an asterisk (*) before a verse indicates that it may, on occasion, be omitted.

Some selections have been labeled "paraphrase" or "metrical paraphrase." If, for example, a canticle does not adhere to the text of The Book of Common Prayer, *The Book of Occasional Services,* or *Supplemental Liturgical Materials,* it is labeled "paraphrase." The term "metrical paraphrase" means that a scriptural text has been restated in a poetic form.

Wonder, Love, and Praise makes use of the term "cantor;" it refers to a person who was, historically, a volunteer leader of prayer in the synagogue. Today it usually refers to someone who has musical ability and who may introduce an antiphon or chant the psalm. A cantor may be anyone in the church who has a strong and pleasant voice, and who can learn to sing the designated parts. A cantor does not have to be a professionally trained singer.

A Leader's Guide is available which duplicates the contents of this book and contains background information about each selection, performance notes, additional accompaniment parts (guitar, handbells, rhythm instruments, etc.), and suggestions for the liturgical use of the music.

Contents

Hymns and Spiritual Songs

Service Music

Indices

Hymns and Spiritual Songs

Signs of endings all around us

1. Signs of end-ings all a - round us dark-ness, death, and win - ter days
2. Can it be that from our end - ings, new be - gin - nings you cre - ate?
3. Speak, O God, your Word a - mong us. Bar - ren lives your pres - ence fill.

shroud our lives in fear and sad - ness, numb-ing mouths that long to praise.
Life from death, and from our rend - ings, realms of whole - ness gen - er - ate?
Swell our hearts with songs of glad-ness, ter - rors calm fore-bod - ings still.

Come, O Christ, and dwell a - mong us! Hear our cries, come set us free.
Take our fears, then, Lord, and turn them in - to hopes for life a - new:
Let your prom-ised realm of jus - tice blos - som now through-out the earth;

Give us hope and faith and glad-ness. Show us what there yet can be.
Fad-ing light and dy-ing sea-son sing their Glo-ri-as to you.
your do-min-ion bring now near us; we a-wait the sav-ing birth.

Words: Dean W. Nelson (b. 1944) © 1988 Dean W. Nelson
Music: *Ton-y-Botel*, Thomas John Williams (1869-1944)

87.87.D

722 The desert shall rejoice

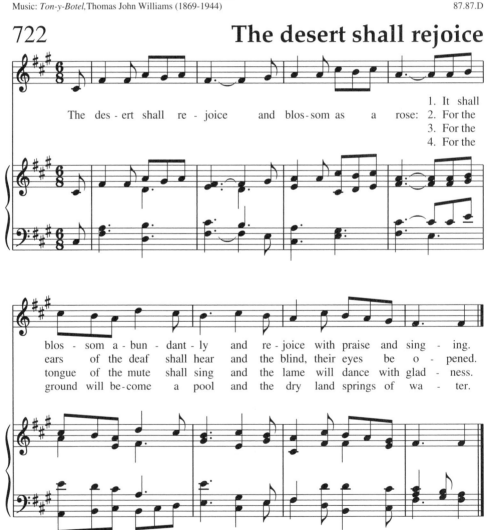

The des-ert shall re-joice and blos-som as a rose:
1. It shall
2. For the
3. For the
4. For the

blos-som a-bun-dant-ly and re-joice with praise and sing-ing.
ears of the deaf shall hear and the blind, their eyes be o-pened.
tongue of the mute shall sing and the lame will dance with glad-ness.
ground will be-come a pool and the dry land springs of wa-ter.

5. The desert shall rejoice
   and blossom as a rose:
   as the ransomed return to God
   and come singing back to Zion.

6. The desert shall rejoice
   and blossom as a rose:
   unto Zion we come with joy,
   for our God has come to save us.

Words: Gracia Grindal (b. 1943) © 1983 Hope Publishing Co.
Music: *Sterling,* Joy F. Patterson (b. 1931) © 1990 Hope Publishing Co., Carol Stream, IL 60188.
   You must contact Hope Publishing Co. to reproduce this selection.

66.88

Isaiah the prophet has written of old 723

1. I - sa - iah the proph - et has writ - ten of old how
2. Yet na - tions still prey on the meek of the world. And

God's earth - ly king - dom shall come. In - stead of the thorn tree the
con - flict turns par - ent from child. Your peo - ple de - spoil all the

fir tree shall grow; the wolf shall lie down with the lamb. The
sweet - ness of earth; the brier and the thorn grow wild. The Lord,

moun - tains and hills shall break forth in - to song, The
has - ten to bring in your king - dom on earth, when

peo - ples be led forth in peace. For the earth shall be filled with the
no one shall hurt or de - stroy. When wis - dom and jus - tice shall

knowl - edge of God as the wa - ters cov - er the seas.
reign in the land and your peo - ple shall go forth in joy.

11.8.11.8 D

724   People, look East

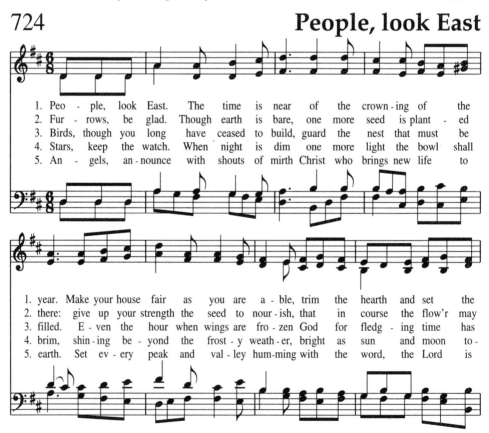

1. Peo - ple, look East. The time is near of the crown - ing of the
2. Fur - rows, be glad. Though earth is bare, one more seed is plant - ed
3. Birds, though you long have ceased to build, guard the nest that must be
4. Stars, keep the watch. When night is dim one more light the bowl shall
5. An - gels, an - nounce with shouts of mirth Christ who brings new life to

1. year. Make your house fair as you are a - ble, trim the hearth and set the
2. there: give up your strength the seed to nour - ish, that in course the flow'r may
3. filled. E - ven the hour when wings are fro - zen God for fledg - ing time has
4. brim, shin - ing be - yond the frost - y weath - er, bright as sun and moon to -
5. earth. Set ev - ery peak and val - ley hum - ming with the word, the Lord is

1. ta - ble. Peo - ple, look East and sing to-day: Love the guest is on the way.
2. flour - ish. Peo - ple, look East and sing to-day: Love the rose is on the way.
3. cho - sen. Peo - ple, look East and sing to-day: Love the bird is on the way.
4. geth - er. Peo - ple, look East and sing to-day: Love the star is on the way.
5. com - ing. Peo - ple, look East and sing to-day: Love the Lord is on the way.

Words: Eleanor Farjeon (1881-1965) © 1957 Eleanor Farjeon; Reprinted by permission of
 Harold Ober Associates, Inc.
Music: *Besançon Carol*, harm. John L. Hooker (b. 1944); harm. © 1997 John L. Hooker

87.98.87

Shengye qing, shengye jing
Holy night, blessed night

725

Sheng - ye qing, sheng - ye jing,
Ho - ly night, bless - ed night,

1. Ming - xing can - lan tian - di ning.
2. Tian - shy xian - xian, mu - ren jing,
3. Jiu - zhu Ye - su jin jiang - sheng;
1. *Stars shine bright - ly, earth is still.*
2. *An - gels sing praise, shep - herds fear,*
3. *Christ has come down, dwells with us.*

Shui su shan mian wan lai wu sheng, qing-yun liao-rao yong zhe Bo - li - heng
jin - qin yu-zheng, man tian he - yun, Ha - li - lu-ya shan - hai yu qi - ming.
bo - ai, xi-sheng, gong-yi, he - ping sheng rong he - hua you ru ry chu-sheng.
Hills and val-leys, field and wood-lands, all sur-round the small town Beth-le-hem.
earth and heav-en ring with prais-es, "Al-le-lu-ia" all cre-a-tion sings.
Sac-ri-fice, love, peace, and jus-tice shine up-on us like the morn-ing sun.

ke - dian ma - cao dan-sheng tian - ing.
Chuan - bao jia - in: Jiu - zhu jiang - sheng.
En - guang hui - yao, zhao-che qian - kun!
In a man-ger Christ the Lord sleeps.
Tell the good news: Christ is born now.
Grace and glo-ry bless the whole world.

Words: Weiyu Zhu and Jingren Wu, 1921; © 1985 Chinese New Hymnal, Chinese Christian Council;
para. Kathleen Moody; © Kathleen Moody
Music: *Sheng Ye Jing* Qigui Shi, 1982; arr. I-to Loh, 1982; © I-to Loh

78.98 with refrain

726   Where is this stupendous stranger?

1. Where is this stu - pen - dous stran - ger? Gen - tle shep - herd now, ad - vise.
2. O the mag - ni - tude of meek - ness! Worth from worth im - mor - tal sprung;

Lead me to my Mas - ter's man - ger, show me where my Sav - ior lies.
O the strength of in - fant weak - ness, if e - ter - nal is so young!

O Most Migh - ty! O Most Ho - ly! Far be - yond the ser - aph's thought,
God all - bount - eous, all - cre - a - tive, whom no ills from good dis - uade,

Ped.

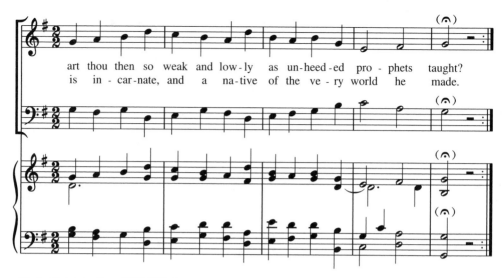

art thou then so weak and low-ly as un-heed-ed pro-phets taught?
is in-car-nate, and a na-tive of the ve-ry world he made.

Words: Christopher Smart (1722-1771) alt.
Music: *Mariposa,* Conrad Susa (b. 1935);
© 1992 E.C. Schirmer Music Company, Inc., a division of ECS Publishing

87.87

727 As panting deer desire the waterbrooks

1. As pant-ing deer de-sire the wa-ter-brooks
2. Both day and night my tears have been my food,
3. Why are you heav-y-heart-ed, O my soul?

when wan-dering in a dry and des-ert place, so yearns my thrist-y soul for
while scof-fers taunt me, "Where is your God now?" My soul dis-solves as I re-
And why are you so mired in deep dis-cord? Still put your hope and trust in

you, O God, and longs at last to see you face to face.
call the throng whose pil-grim hymns I led to Zi-on's brow.
God a-lone, whom I will praise, my Sav-ior and my Lord.

10.10.10.10

Mantos y palmas esparciendo 728
Filled with excitement

1. Man - tos y pal - mas es - par - cien - do va
2. Co - mo en la en - tra - da de Je - ru - sa - lén,
1. *Filled with ex - cite - ment, all the hap - py throng*
2. *As in that en - trance to Je - ru - sa - lem,*

el pue - blo a - le - gre de Je - ru - sa - lén. A - llá a lo le - jos se vis-
to - dos can - ta - mos a Je - sús el Rey, al Cris - to vi - vo que nos
spread cloaks and branch - es on the cit - y streets. There in the dis - tance they be-
ho - san - nas we will sing to Je - sus Christ, To our Re - deem - er who still

lum - bra ya en un po - lli - no al Sal - va - dor Je - sús.
lla - ma hoy pa - ra se - guir - le con a - mor y fe.
gin to see, there on a don - key, comes the Sav - ior, Christ.
calls to - day, asks us to fol - low with our love and faith.

"¡Ho - san - na! ¡Ho - san - na al Rey!"
Ho - san - na, ho - san - na to Christ!"

Words: Rubèn Ruiz Avila (b. 1945); trans. Gertrude C. Suppe, alt. 1987
Music: *Hosanna,* Rubèn Ruiz Avila (b. 1945); arr. Alvin Schutmaat
© 1972, 1979, 1989 The United Methodist Publishing House

10.10.10.10 with refrain

As in that upper room
you left your seat

729

1. As in that up-per room you left your seat and took a towel and
2. I bow be-fore you, all my sin con-fessed, to hear a-gain the
3. So in re-mem-brance of your life laid down I come to praise you

chose a ser-vant's part, so for to - day, Lord, wash a - gain my
words of love you said; and at your ta - ble, as your hon - ored
for your grace di - vine; Saved by your cross, and sub - ject to your

feet, who in your mer - cy died to cleanse my heart.
guest, I take and eat the true and liv - ing bread.
crown, strength - ened for ser - vice by this bread and wine.

Words: Timothy Dudley-Smith (b. 1926); © 1993 Hope Publishing Co.,
    Carol Stream, IL, 60188. All rights reserved. Used by permission.
Music: *Sursum Corda,* Alfred Morton Smith (1879-1971); © Church of the Ascension, Atlantic City, NJ.
    You must contact Hope Publishing Co. to reproduce these words.

10.10.10.10

As in that upper room you left your seat

1. As in that up-per room you left your seat
2. I bow be-fore you, all my sin con - fessed,
3. So in re-mem-brance of your life laid down

and took a towel and chose a ser-vant's part, so for to - day, Lord,
to hear a - gain the words of love you said; and at your ta - ble,
I come to praise you for your grace di - vine; saved by your cross, and

wash a - gain my feet, who in your mer - cy died to cleanse my
as your hon - oured guest, I take and eat the true and liv - ing
sub - ject to your crown, strength-ened for ser - vice by this bread and

heart.
Bread.
wine.

2. I
3. So

Three holy days enfold us now   731

1. Three ho-ly days en-fold us now in wash-ing
2. The myst'-ry hid from ag-es past is here re-
3. Christ lift-ed high up-on the tree, be-fore you

feet and break-ing bread, in cross and font and
vealed in word and sign, for Je-sus' sto-ry
ev-ery knee shall bend and ev-ery tongue in

life re-newed: in Christ, God's first-born from the dead.
is our own: new life through death is God's de-sign.
praise pro-claim: "You are the Lord of all. A-men."

732   Three holy days enfold us now

1. Three ho - ly days en - fold us now in wash - ing
2. The my - st'ry hid from a - ges past is here re -
3. Christ lift - ed high up - on the tree, be - fore you

feet and break - ing bread, in cross and font and
vealed in word and sign, for Je - sus' sto - ry
ev - 'ry knee shall bend and ev - 'ry tongue in

life re - newed: In Christ, God's first - born from the dead.
is our own: new life through death is God's de - sign.
praise pro - claim: "You are the Lord of all. A - men."

Words: Delores Dufner, OSB (b.1939); © 1995 Sisters of St. Benedict
Music: *Lux vera lucis radium*; Mode I; ed. Mason Martens (1933-1991) © 1984 Mason Martens

733   Three holy days enfold us now

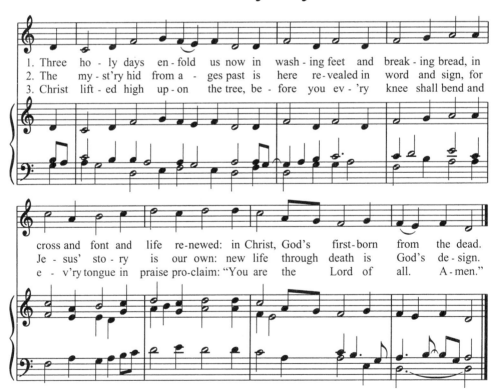

1. Three ho - ly days en - fold us now in wash - ing feet and break - ing bread, in
2. The my - st'ry hid from a - ges past is here re - vealed in word and sign, for
3. Christ lift - ed high up - on the tree, be - fore you ev - 'ry knee shall bend and

cross and font and life re - newed: in Christ, God's first - born from the dead.
Je - sus' sto - ry is our own: new life through death is God's de - sign.
e - v'ry tongue in praise pro - claim: "You are the Lord of all. A - men."

Words: Delores Dufner, OSB (b. 1939); © 1995 Sisters of St. Benedict
Music: *Lux vera lucis radium;* Setting Monte Mason (b. 1949); acc. © 1996 Monte Mason   LM

You laid aside your rightful reputation 734

1. You laid a - side your right - ful rep - u - ta - tion
2. You touched the lep - er, ate with those re - ject - ed,
3. Help us to fol - low, Je - sus, where you lead us
4. Draw us to you and with your love trans - form us:

and gave no heed to what the world might say;
re - ceived the wor - ship of a wo - man's tears:
to love, to serve, our own lives lay - ing down;
the love we've seen, the love we've touched and known;

served as a slave and laid a - side your gar - ments
You shed the pride that keeps us from the free - dom
to walk your way of hum - ble, cost - ly ser - vice,
en - large our hearts and with com - pas - sion fill us

to wash the feet of those who walked your way.
to love our neigh - bor, lay - ing down our fears.
a cross its end, a ring of thorns its crown.
to love, to serve, to fol - low you a - lone.

Words: Rosalind Brown (b. 1953)

© 1992 CELEBRATION, Aliquippa, PA 15001. All rights reserved. International copyright secured. Used by permission.
You must contact CELEBRATION to reproduce these words.

Music: *Intercessor*, Charles Hubert Hastings Parry (1848–1918)

O sacred head, sore wounded

1. O sa - cred head, sore wound - ed, _____
2. Thy beau - ty, long de - sir - ed, _____
3. In thy most bit - ter pas - sion _____
* 4. What lan - guage shall I bor - row _____
* 5. My days are few, O fail not, _____

_____ de - filed and put to scorn;
_____ hath van - ished from our sight;
_____ my heart to share doth cry,
_____ to thank thee, dear - est friend,
_____ with thine im - mor - tal power,

O king - ly head. sur -
thy power is all ex -
with thee for my sal -
for this thy dy - ing
to hold me that I

death thy bloom de - flower?
not so far thy grace,
stand thy cross be - neath,
should I faint - ing be,
see in my last strife

O coun - te - nance whose splen - dor
show me, O Love most high - est,
to mourn thee, well - be - lov - ed,
Lord, let me nev - er, nev - er,
to me thine arms ex - tend - ed

the hosts of heav'n a dore!
the bright - ness of thy face.
yet thank thee for thy death.
out - live my love for thee.
up - on the cross of life.

Words: Paulus Gerhard (1607-1676)
Music: *Redding*, David Hurd (b. 1950) © 1992 GIA Publications, Inc.
You must contact GIA Publications, Inc. to reproduce this music.

76.76.D

1. When Je-sus came to Gol-go-tha they
2. When Je-sus came to live with us we
3. Still Je-sus cries, "For-give them for they

hanged him on a tree, they drove great nails through hands and feet, and
sim - ply passed him by, we nev - er hurt a hair of him, we
know not what they do," and still it rains the win - ter rain that

made a Cal - va - ry; they crowned him with a crown of thorns,
on - ly let him die; for we had grown more ten - der, and we
drench - es through and through; the crowds go home and leave the streets with -

red were his wounds and deep, for those were crude and cru - el days, and
would not give him pain, we on - ly just passed down the street and
out a soul to see, and Je - sus crouch - es 'gainst a wall and

1. 2.

hu - man flesh was cheap.
left him in the rain.

3.

3. cries for Cal - va - ry.

Words: Geoffrey Anketel Studdert-Kennedy (1883-1929)
Music: *Indifference*, Alec Wyton (b. 1921); © 1988 Roger Dean Publishing Company,
a division of the Lorenz Corp., Dayton, OH. All rights reserved.
Reproduced by permission - License # 413702

14.14.14.14

737   Faithful cross, above all other
Crux fidelis inter omnes

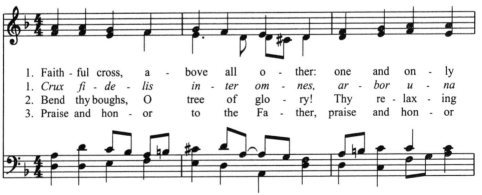

1. Faith - ful cross, a - bove all o - ther: one and on - ly
1. *Crux fi - de - lis in - ter om - nes, ar - bor u - na*
2. Bend thy boughs, O tree of glo - ry! Thy re - lax - ing
3. Praise and hon - or to the Fa - ther, praise and hon - or

Words: Venantius Honorius Fortunatus (540-600?) tr. ver. *Hymnal 1982* after John Mason Neale (1818-1866)
© Church Pension Fund

Music: *Monrovia*, Randall Giles (b. 1950); © 1994 Paraclete Press

87.87.87

Day of delight and beauty unbounded 738

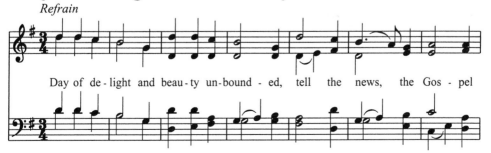

spread! Day of all won - der, day of all splen - dor, tell Christ ris - en

from the dead!

1. Sing of the sun from dark-ness ap-pear-ing, sing of the
Sing of the stream from Je - sus' side flow-ing; sing of the
2. Sing now of mourn-ing turned in -to danc-ing, sing now the
Sing now of fast - ing turned in -to feast-ing, sing the Lord's

seed from bar - ren earth green - ing, sing of cre - a - tion, al - le - lu - ia!
saints in wa - ter made ho - ly; sing of sal - va - tion, al - le - lu - ia!
mys - t'ry, hope of our glo - ry, sing with thanks-giv - ing, al - le - lu - ia!
fav - or last-ing for - ev - er; sing all things liv - ing, al - le - lu - ia!

Refrain after each stanza

Words: Delores Dufner, OSB (b. 1939); © 1996 Sisters of St. Benedict
Music: *In dir ist Freude*, Giovanni Gastoldi, (1556-1622); harm. John L. Hooker (b. 1944);
    harm. © 1997 John L. Hooker

10.7.10.7 10.10.9D

739   Camina, pueblo de Dios
Walk on, O people of God

Estribillo, Unisono
(Refrain, Unison)

Ca - mi - na, pue-blo de Dios, ca - mi - na, pue-blo de Dios, Nue - va
Walk on, O peo-ple of God; walk on, O peo-ple of God! A new

ley, nue - va a - lian - za, en la nue - va cre - a - ción. Ca -
law, God's new al - li - ance, all cre - a - tion is re - born. Walk

Fine

mi - na, pue - blo de Dios, ca - mi - na, pue - blo de Dios.
on, O peo - ple of God; walk on, O peo - ple of God!

1. Mi - ra a - llá en el Cal - va - rio en la ro - ca hay u - na cruz;
2. Cris - to to - ma en su cuer - po el pe - ca - do, la es - cla - vi - tud.
1. Look on Cal - va - ry's sum - mit; on the rock there tow - ers a cross;
2. Christ takes in - to his bod - y all our sin, en - slave - ment, and pain;

muer - te que en - gen - dra la vi - da, es - pe - ran - za nue - va luz.
Al des - tru - ir - los, nos tra - e u - na nue - va ple - ni - tud.
death that gives birth to new liv - ing, a new peo - ple, a new light.
as he de - stroys them he brings us life's a - bun - dance, life's new joy.

3. Cielo y tierra se abrazan,
   nuestra alma halla el perdón.
   Vuelven a abrirse los cielos
   para el mundo pecador.
   Israel peregrino,
   vive y canta tu redención.
   Hay nuevos mundos abiertos
   en la nueva creación.
      Estribillo

3. *Heav'n and earth are embracing,*
   and our souls find pardon at last.
   Now heaven's gates are reopened
   to the sinner, to us all.
   Israel walks a journey;
   now we live, salvation's our song;
   Christ's resurrection has freed us.
   There are new worlds to explore.
      Refrain

Words: Cesáreo Gabaraín (1936-1991), tr. George Lockwood, © 1989 United Methodist Publishing House
Music: *Nueva Creación,* Cesáreo Gabaraín (1936-1991); © 1979 Cesáreo Gabaraín.
     Published by OCP Publications, 5536 NE Hassalo, Portland, OR 97213.
     All rights reserved. Used with permission. harm. Juan Luis Garcia
     You must contact OCP Publications to reproduce this selection.
78.78.D with refrain

740   Wade in the water

Fine

Wade in the wa - ter, God's a-gon-na trou-ble the wa - ter.

1. See that host all dressed in white,
2. See that band all dressed in red,
3. Look o - ver yon - der, what do I see?
4. If you don't be - lieve I've been re - deemed,

God's a - gon - na trou - ble the

wa - ter.

1. The lead - er looks like the Is - ra - elite,
2. Looks like the band that Mo - ses led,
3. The Ho - ly Ghost a - com - ing on me,
4. Just fol - low me down to Jor - dan's stream,

D.C.

God's a - gon - na trou - ble the wa - ter.

Words: Traditional
Music: Negro Spiritual; arr. Carl Haywood (b. 1949), from *The Haywood Collection of Negro Spirituals*
© 1992 Carl Haywood
You must contact Carl Haywood to reproduce this selection.

Irr.

741 Filled with the Spirit's power

1. Filled with the Spir - it's power, with one ac - cord
2. Now with the mind of Christ set us on fire,
3. Wid - en our love, good Spir - it, to em - brace

the in - fant church con - fessed its ris - en Lord.
that u - ni - ty may be our great de - sire.
in your strong care all those of ev - ery race.

O Ho - ly Spir - it, in the church to - day
Give joy and peace; give faith to hear your call,
Like wind and fire with life a - mong us move,

no less your power of fel - low - ship dis - play.
and read - i - ness in each to work for all.
till we are known as Christ's, and Chris - tians prove.

Words: J.R. Peacey (1896-1971); © 1978 Hope Publishing Co., Carol Stream, IL 60188
        All rights reserved. Used by permission.
Music: *Ashley*, David Ashley White (b. 1944); ©1996 Selah Publishing Co., Inc.
        You must contact Hope Publishing to reproduce these words, and Selah Publishing Co., Inc. to reproduce the music.

10.10.10.10

Loving Spirit 742

1. Lov - ing Spir - it, lov - ing Spir - it, you have cho - sen me to be;
2. Like a moth - er you en - fold me, hold my life with - in your own.
3. Like a fa - ther you pro - tect me. Teach me the dis - cern - ing eye.
4. Friend and lov - er in your close - ness I am known and held and blest:
5. Lov - ing Spir - it, lov - ing Spir - it, you have cho - sen me to be;

you have drawn me to your won - der, you have set your sign on me.
Feed me with your ver - y bod - y, form me of your flesh and bone.
Hoist me up up - on your shoul - der, let me see the world from high.
in your prom - ise is my com - fort, in your pres - ence I may rest.
you have drawn me to your won - der, you have set your sign on me.

Words: Shirley Erena Murray (b. 1931); © 1987 The Hymn Society. All rights reserved.
Used by permission of Hope Publishing Co., Carol Stream, IL 60188.
Music: *Omni die*, melody from *Gross Catolisch Gesangbuch*, 1631; harm. William Smith Rockstro (1823-1895)
You must contact Hope Publishing Co. to reproduce these words.

8 7.8 7

O threefold God of tender unity 743

1. O three-fold God of ten - der u - ni - ty, life's great un-known that
2. O blaze of ra - diance, source of light that blinds, the fie - ry splen - dor
3. Most lov - ing Par - ent, Child of joys and pains cre - a - tive Spi - rit,
4. In ev - 'ry mak - ing, each cre - a - tive dream and in the flow of
5. O three-fold God of ten - der u - ni - ty, life's great un-known that

binds and sets us free: felt in our lov-ing, great-er than our thought,
of pro-phe-tic minds, you live in mys-tery, yet with-in us dwell;
life-force that sus-tains, in bone and flesh, we touch your gen-tle hand,
life's great heal-ing stream, when love is born or peo-ple re-con-ciled,
binds and sets us free: felt in our lov-ing, great-er than our thought,

you are the mys-tery found, the mys - tery sought.
life springs from you as from a liv - ing well.
your face we see in wa - ter, air, and land.
we share your life, O Par - ent, Spi - rit, Child.
you are the mys-tery found, the mys - tery sought.

Words: W.L. Wallace (b.1933); © 1988 by W.L. Wallace
Used by permission of Hope Publishing Co., Carol Stream, IL 60188
Music: *Flentge*, Carl Flentge Schalk (b. 1929); © 1979 GIA Publications, Inc.
You must contact Hope Publishing to reproduce these words and
GIA Publications, Inc. to reproduce this music .

10.10.10.10

744   O Trinity of blessed light

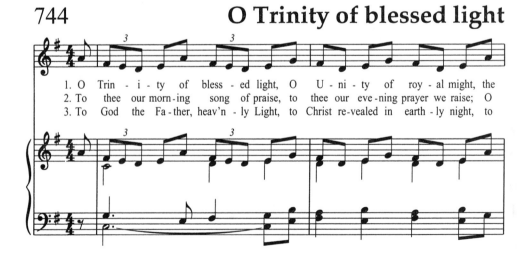

1. O Trin - i - ty of bless - ed light, O U - ni - ty of roy - al might, the
2. To thee our morn-ing song of praise, to thee our eve -ning prayer we raise; O
3. To God the Fa - ther, heav'n - ly Light, to Christ re-vealed in earth - ly night, to

fier - y sun now goes its way; shed thou with - in our hearts thy ray.
grant us with thy saints on high to praise thee through e - ter - ni - ty.
God the Ho - ly Ghost we raise our e - qual and un - ceas - ing praise.

Words: Latin, 6th cent.; tr. John Mason Neale (1818-1866), St. 3 Charles Coffin (1676-1749);
      tr. John Chandler (1806-1876) alt.
Music: *St. Martin*, James Woodman (b. 1957); © 1997 Church Pension Fund.   LM

God, beyond all human praises   745

Descant

You _____ are the Ho - ly One.

1. God, be - yond all hu - man prais - es, wings of cher - u -
2. God of har - mo - ny and beau - ty, God of floods by
3. God of his - tory's plan un - fold - ing, jus - tice as its
4. Hu - man sin your plan has twist - ed, hu - man wills de -

You _____ are the

bim your throne, hid by light's en - gulf - ing splen - dor,
tem - pest blown, God of Na - ture's jea - lous or - der,
goal and crown; God of free - dom, God of mys - t'ry,
fy your own; all the world re - verts to cha - os.

Ho - ly One, the Ho - ly One. You are the Ho-ly One.

rule in heav'n as God a - lone. You are the Ho - ly One.
rule on earth as God a - lone. You are the Ho - ly One.
rule through time as God a - lone. You are the Ho - ly One.
Rule and judge as God a - lone. You are the Ho - ly One.

5. You, by Jesus' Cross and Passion, made in hope creation one.
   Now we live by your forgiveness.
   Rule in love as Love alone.
   You are the Holy One.

6. Keep us ever in your presence; in your Love our love has grown.
   Wash us, feed us, turn us, heal us,
   rule our hearts through Love alone.
   You are the Holy One.

* 7. God of all our new beginnings, seal with grace what we have done.
   Bless our Bishop, bless *her* people.
   Rule your church through Love alone.
   You are the Holy One.

8. Lead us onward to your kingdom on the way your Love makes known.
   God, our joy, our peace, our glory,
   Holy Love you rule alone.
   You are the Holy One.

Words: Charles P. Price (b. 1920); © 1993 Charles P. Price
Music: *Dominus regnavit*, Richard Wayne Dirksen (b. 1921); © 1993 Richard Wayne Dirksen   87.87 with refrain

God the sculptor of the mountains 746

1. God the sculp-tor of the moun-tains, God the mil - ler of the sand,
2. God the nui-sance to the Pha - raoh, God the cleav - er of the sea,
3. God the un - ex-pect - ed in - fant, God the calm, de - ter-mined youth,
4. God the dress-er of the vine - yard, God the plant - er of the wheat,

God the jewel - er of the heav - ens, God the pot - ter of the land:
God the pil - lar of the dark - ness, God the bea - con of the free:
God the ta - ble turn-ing pro - phet, God the res - ur-rect-ed Truth:
God the reap-er of the har - vest, God the source of all we eat:

you are womb of all cre - a - tion, we are form - less; shape us now.
you are gate of all de - liv' - rance, we are sight-less; lead us now.
you are pres-ent ev - ery mo - ment, we are search-ing; meet us now.
you are host at ev - ery ta - ble, we are hun - gry; feed us now.

Words: John Thornburg (b. 1954); © 1994 John Thornburg
Music: *Sandria*, Gerre Hancock (b. 1934) © Oxford University Press

87. 87.87

747 God the sculptor of the mountains

1. God the sculp-tor of the moun-tains, God the mil-ler of the sand,
2. God the nui-sance to the Pha-raoh, God the cleav-er of the sea,
3. God the un-ex-pect-ed in-fant, God the calm, de-ter-mined Youth,
4. God the dress-er of the vine-yard, God the plant-er of the wheat,

God the jewel-er of the heav-ens, God the pot-ter of the land:
God the pil-lar of the dark-ness, God the bea-con of the free:
God the ta-ble turn-ing pro-phet, God the res-ur-rect-ed Truth:
God the reap-er of the har-vest, God the source of all we eat:

you are womb of all cre-a-tion, we are form-less; shape us now.
you are gate of all de-liv'-rance, we are sight-less; lead us now.
you are pres-ent ev-ery mo-ment, we are search-ing; meet us now.
you are host at ev-ery ta-ble, we are hun-gry; feed us now.

Words: John Thornburg (b. 1954); © 1994 John Thornburg
Music: *Urbs beata,* Sarum Plainsong, Mode II, Hymnal 1940 © 1941, 1943, 1961, 1981
    Church Pension Fund

87.87.87

From the dawning of creation 748

1. From the dawn - ing of cre - a - tion, God was pres - ent in the Word.
2. Light ap-peared in deep - est dark-ness. Night was end - ed, morn - ing dawned.
3. Hu - man eyes have seen God's glo - ry; hu - man hands have touched God's own.

And the Word was God e - ter - nal, source of all that came to be.
And that light is ev - er burn - ing, bright-ness nev - er o - ver - come.
In our like - ness here a - mong us, dwells the Word of God made flesh.

Je - sus is that Word e - ter - nal. Je - sus is the Word of life.
Je - sus is that Light e - ter - nal. Je - sus is the Word of life.
Je - sus is that Word in - car - nate. Je - sus is the Word of life.

Words: Delores Dufner, OSB (b. 1939); © 1988 Sisters of St. Benedict
Music: *Timeless Love,* Norman Warren (b. 1934); © 1973 Hope Publishing Co., Carol Stream, IL 60188.
  All rights reserved. Used by permission.
  You must contact Hope Publishing Co. to reproduce this music. 87.87.87

The tree of life my soul hath seen

1. The tree of life my soul hath seen, La - den with fruit, and al - ways green: The trees of na - ture fruit - less be Com - pared with Christ the ap - ple tree.
2. His beau - ty doth all things ex - cel: By faith I know, but ne'er can tell the glo - ry which I now can see In Je - sus
3. For hap - pi - ness I long have sought, And pleas - ure dear - ly I have bought: I missed of all: but now I see 'Tis found in
4. I'm wear - y with my for - mer toil, Here I will sit and rest a while: Un - der the shad - ow I will be Of Je - sus
5. This fruit doth make my soul to thrive, It keeps my dy - ing faith a - live; Which makes my soul in haste to be With Je - sus

Words: Anonymous, from a collection of Joshua Smith, New Hampshire, 1784
Music: *Apple Tree*, Daniel Pinkham (b. 1923)
© 1990 Ione Press, Inc., a division of ECS Publishing

LM

So the day dawn for me

1. So the day dawn for me, so the day break,
2. Be the day shine for me, be the day bright,

Christ watch - ing o - ver me, Christ as I wake.
Christ my com - pan - ion be, Christ be my light. *to vs. 3*

3. Be the day dark to me, be the day drear,
4. Be the day swift to me, be the day long,

Christ shall my com - fort be, Christ be my cheer.
Christ my con - tent - ment be, Christ be my song. *to vs. 5*

5. So the day close for me, so the night fall,

Christ watch-ing o - ver me, Christ be my all.

751 Ev'ry time I feel the spirit

Harmony

Ev' - ry time I feel the spir - it, mov - ing

in my heart, I will pray. Ev - ry time I feel the

Fine

spir - it, mov - ing in my heart, I will pray.

unison

1. Up on the moun - tain   my Lord spoke,   out of his
2. Jor - dan ri - ver   chil- ly and cold,   chills the

mouth came fire and smoke. All a-round me looked so
bod - y but not the soul. There ain't but one train so runs this

fine, asked my Lord if all was mine.
track, runs to heav - en and runs right back.

D.C.

Words: Traditional
Music: Negro Spiritual

Irr.

There's a sweet, sweet Spirit in this place   752

1. There's a sweet, sweet Spir - it in this place, _____ and I
(2. There are) bless - ings you can-not re - ceive _____ till you
(3. If you) say he saved you from your sin, _____ now you're

know that it's the Spir - it of the Lord._____ There are
know him in his full - ness, and be - lieve._____ You're the
weak, you're bound, and can - not en - ter in,_____ you can

sweet ex - pres - sions on each face,_____ and I
one to pro - fit when you say,_____ "I am
make it right if you will yield;_____ you'll en -

know they feel the pres - ence of the Lord._____
going to walk with Je - sus all the way."_____
joy the Ho - ly Spir - it that we feel._____

been re - vived when we shall leave this place. 2. There are
3. If you place.

Words: Doris Akers (1922-1995)
Music: Doris Akers (1922-1995)
© 1962, renewed 1990 MANNA MUSIC, INC.

64.64

753 When from bondage we are summoned

1. When from bond - age we are sum-moned out of dark-ness in - to light,
2. When our God names us a peo - ple, Je - sus leads us by the hand
3. Through all stag - es of the jour - ney Christ is with us, night and day,
4. We must not lose sight of Je - sus, who ac - cept - ed pain and loss,
5. See the prize our God has prom-ised: end - less life with Christ our Lord.

1. we must go in hope and pat - ience, walk by faith and not by sight.
2. through a lone - ly, bar - ren des - ert to a great and glo - rious land.
3. with com - pas - sion for our weak - ness ev - 'ry step a - long the way.
4. who, for joy of love un - meas - ured, dared em-brace the shame - ful cross.
5. Now we fix our eyes on Je - sus, walk by faith in Je - sus' word.

Let us throw off all that hin-ders; let us run the race to win!

Let us hast-en to our home-land and, re-joic-ing, en-ter in. _____

Words: Delores Dufner, OSB (b. 1939); © 1984, 1988, and 1996 Sisters of St. Benedict
Music: *Grid*, Thomas Pavlechko (b. 1962); © 1995 Thomas Pavlechko

87.87 D

When from bondage we are summoned 754

1. When   from bon - dage
2. When   our   God names
3. Through all   stag - es
4. We   must not lose
5. See   the   prize our

has - ten to our home - land and, re - joic - ing, en - ter in. in.

Words: Delores Dufner, OSB (b. 1939); © 1894, 1988, 1996 Sisters of St. Benedict
Music: *Haywood's Home,* Carl Haywood (b. 1949), from *Tunes for Grace;*
     © 1997 Carl Haywood
     You must contact Carl Haywood to reproduce this music.

87.87 D

The steadfast love of the Lord never ceases 755

The stead - fast love of the Lord nev - er ceas - es:

God's mer - cies nev - er come to an end;

they are new ev - ery morn - ing; your

Last time to 🛦

faith - ful - ness O Lord is great.

You are all that I have: and there - fore I will wait for you.

You, O Lord, are good to those who wait for you: to all those who seek you.

It is good to wait in pa-tience for the sal-va-tion of the Lord. God's mer - cies nev - er come to an end. The

CODA

great _____ Your faith-ful-ness O Lord is great. _____

Words: © 1989 *A New Zealand Prayer Book* - He Karakia Mihihare O Aotearoa
Music: Carl Haywood (b. 1949), from *Tunes for Grace;* © 1997 Carl Haywood

Irr.

Lead me, guide me, along the way

Lead me, guide me, a-long the way,
For if you lead me, I can-not stray.
Lord, let me walk each day with Thee.
Lead me, Oh Lord, lead me.

Fine

1. I am weak and I need thy strength and power to
2. Help me tread in the paths of right - eous - ness, be my
3. I am lost if you take your hand from me, I am

help me o - ver my weak - est hour; Help me
aid when sa - tan and sin op - press; I am
blind with - out thy light to see; Lord, just

through the dark - ness thy face to see,
put - ting all my trust in thee.
al - ways let me thy ser - vant be.

D.C.

Lead me, Oh Lord, lead me. _____
Lead me, Oh Lord, lead me. _____
Lead me, Oh Lord, lead me. _____

Words: Doris M. Akers (1922-1995)
Music: Doris M. Akers (1922-1995); arr. Richard Smallwood
© 1953 Doris Akers. Copyright Renewed. All Rights admin.
Unichappel Music, Inc. Intenational Copyright Secured. All Rights Reserved.
You must contact Hal Leonard Corporation to reproduce this selection.   Irr.

757 Will you come and follow me

1. Will you come and fol - low me if I but call your name? Will you go where you don't know and nev - er be the same? Will you let my love be shown? Will you
2. Will you leave your self be - hind if I but call your name? Will you care for cruel and kind and nev - er be the same? Will you risk the hos - tile stare should your
3. Will you let the blind - ed see if I but call your name? Will you set the pris - 'ner free and nev - er be the same? Will you kiss the lep - er clean, and do
4. Will you love the "You" you hide if I but call your name? Will you quell the fear in - side and nev - er be the same? Will you use the faith you've found to re -
5. Christ, your sum - mons ech - oes true when you but call my name. Let me turn and fol - low you and nev - er be the same. In your com - pa - ny I'll go where your

let my Name be known? Will you let my life be grown in
life at - tract or scare? Will you let me an - swer prayer in
such as this un - seen? And ad - mit to what I mean in
shape the world a - round through my sight and touch and sound in
love and foot - steps show, thus I'll move and live and grow in

1, 2, 3, 4.

you and you in me?
you and you in me?
you and you in me?
you and you in me?

5. (Final ending)

5. you and you in me.

Words: from the Iona Community; © 1989 GIA Publications
Music: *Mary Alexandra*, John L. Hooker (b. 1944); © 1996 John L. Hooker
You must contact GIA Publications, Inc. to reproduce these words.

13.13.7.7.13

Tú has venido a la orilla   758
You have come down to the lakeshore

1. Tú _____ has ve - ni - do a la o - ri - lla, _____ no has bus-
2. Tú _____ sa - bes bien lo que ten - go: _____ en mi
1. *You _____ have come down to the lake - shore _____ seek - ing*
2. *You _____ know full well my pos - ses - sions. _____ Nei - ther*

ca - do _____ ni a sa - bios, ni a ri - cos, _____ tan só - lo
bar - ca _____ no hay o - ro ni es - pa - das; _____ tan só - lo
nei - ther _____ the wise nor the weal - thy, _____ But on - ly
trea - sure _____ nor weap - ons for con - quest, _____ Just these my

*Estribillo
(Refrain)*

quie - res _____ que yo te si - ga. _____ Je -
re - des _____ y mi tra - ba - jo. _____ O
ask - ing _____ for me to fol - low. _____ O
fish nets _____ and will for work - ing. _____

sús, _____ me has mi - ra - do a los o - jos; _____ son - ri -
Je - sus, _____ you have looked in - to my eyes; _____ kind - ly

en - do _____ has di - cho mi nom - bre; _____ en la a -
smil - ing, _____ you've called out my name. _____ On the

re - na _____ he de-ja-do mi bar - ca; _____ jun-to a
sand I _____ have a-ban-doned my small boat; _____ now with

ti _____ bus-ca-ré o-tro mar. _____
you, _____ I will seek oth-er seas. _____

3. Tú necesitas mis manos,
   mi cansancio que a otros descanse,
   amor que quiera seguir amando.
   Estribillo

3. *You need my hands, my exhaustion,*
   working love for the rest of the weary
   A love that's willing to go on loving.
   Refrain

4. Tú, Pescador de otros mares,
   ansia eterna de almas que esperan.
   Amigo bueno, que así me llamas.
   Estribillo

4. *You who have fished other waters;*
   you, the longing of souls that
   are yearning:
   As loving Friend, you have come to call me.
   Refrain

Words: Cesáreo Gabaraín, (1936-1991), alt., trans. Madeleine F. Marshall, alt.
Music: *Pescador*, Cesáreo Gabaraín, (1936-1991), alt., harm. Skinner Chávez-Melo
(1944-1992); harm. © Skinner Chávez-Melo
© 1979, 1987, 1989 Cesáreo Gabaraín. Published by OCP Publications, 5536 NE
Hassalo, Portland, OR 97213. All rights reserved. Used with permission.
You must contact OCP Publications to reproduce this selection.   Irr.

With awe approach the mysteries   759

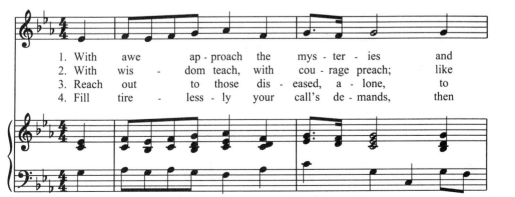

1. With   awe   ap - proach the   mys - ter - ies   and
2. With   wis - dom teach, with cou - rage preach;   like
3. Reach   out   to those   dis - eased, a - lone,   to
4. Fill   tire - less - ly   your   call's de - mands, then

wres - tle with the Word like Ja - cob, bruised yet
Deb - orah, lead your flock in - side the cul - ture's
those con - fused, op - posed; and like a mo - ther,
rest, like Christ, a - part, re - freshed by God's re -

strange - ly blest. Ser - vant - hood is pain.
dan - ger zone. Ser - vant - hood is faith.
heal, for - give. Ser - vant - hood is grace.
new - ing strength. Ser - vant - hood is love.

Words: Jane Manton Marshall (b. 1924)
Music: *Helensong*, Jane Manton Marshall (b. 1924)

86.85

760 O wheat whose crushing was for bread

1. O wheat, whose crush - ing was for bread, O
2. O fruit whose crush - ing was for wine, O
3. O life whose crush - ing was for love, O

bread whose break - ing is for life, O life, your seem - ing end is
wine whose flow - ing is for blood, O blood, your pour - ing out is
love whose spend - ing was to death, O death, your mourn - ning is our

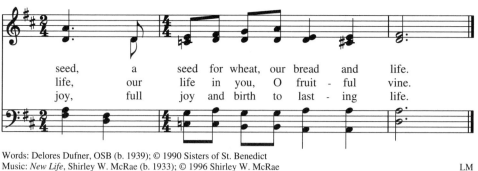

seed, a seed for wheat, our bread and life.
life, our life in you, O fruit - ful vine.
joy, full joy and birth to last - ing life.

Words: Delores Dufner, OSB (b. 1939); © 1990 Sisters of St. Benedict
Music: *New Life*, Shirley W. McRae (b. 1933); © 1996 Shirley W. McRae   LM

All who hunger gather gladly   761

1. All who hun - ger gath - er glad - ly; ho - ly man - na
2. All who hun - ger, nev - er stran - gers, seek - er, be a
3. All who hun - ger, sing to - geth - er, Je - sus Christ is

is our bread. Come from wil - der - ness and wan - d'ring.
wel - come guest. Come from rest - less - ness and roam - ing.
liv - ing bread. Come from lone - li - ness and long - ing.

Here in truth we will be fed. You that yearn for
Here, in joy we keep the feast. We that once were
Here, in peace, we have been fed. Blest are those who

days of full - ness, all a - round us is our food.
lost and scat - tered in com - mun - ion's love have stood.
from this ta - ble live their days in grat - i - tude.

Taste and see the grace e - ter - nal.
Taste and see the grace e - ter - nal.
Taste and see the grace e - ter - nal.

Taste and see that God is good.
Taste and see that God is good.
Taste and see that God is good.

Words: Sylvia G. Dunstan (1955-1993) © 1991, GIA Publications, Inc.
Music: *Holy Manna*, from *The Southern Harmony*, 1835
   You must contact GIA Publications, Inc. to reproduce these words.

Harmony (the melody is in the tenor)

1. All who hun - ger gath - er glad - ly; ho - ly man - na
2. All who hun - ger, nev - er stran - gers, seek - er, be a
3. All who hun - ger, sing to - geth - er, Je - sus Christ is

is our bread. Come from wil - der - ness and wan - d'ring.
wel - come guest. Come from rest - less - ness and roam - ing.
liv - ing bread. Come from lone - li - ness and long - ing.

Here in truth we will be fed. You that yearn for
Here, in joy we keep the feast. We that once were
Here, in peace, we have been fed. Blest are those who

days of full - ness, all a - round us is our food.
lost and scat - tered in com - mun - ion's love have stood.
from this ta - ble live their days in grat - i - tude.

Taste and see the grace e - ter - nal. Taste and see that God is good.
Taste and see the grace e - ter - nal. Taste and see that God is good.
Taste and see the grace e - ter - nal. Taste and see that God is good.

Words: Sylvia G. Dunstan (1955-1993) © 1991, GIA Publications, Inc.
Music: *Holy Manna*, from *Columbian Harmony*, 1825
    You must contact GIA Publications, Inc. to reproduce these words.

87.87.D

I am the bread of life

Descant after stanzas 3 & 4

I am the bread of life, I am the bread of life.

Antiphon

I am the bread of life, I am the bread of life.

1. Who - ev - er comes to me shall nev - er hun - ger,
2. This is the liv - ing Bread which comes from heav - en,
3. None come to me un - less the Fa - ther draw them,
4. All they who eat my flesh and drink my blood

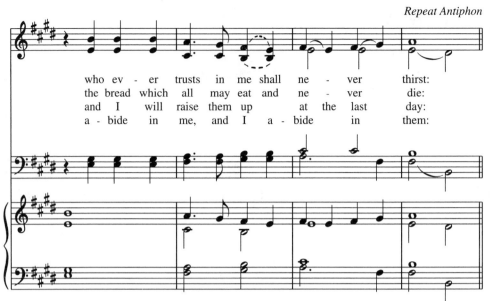

who ev - er trusts in me shall ne - ver thirst:
the bread which all may eat and ne - ver die:
and I will raise them up at the last day:
a - bide in me, and I a - bide in them:

Words: Jack Warren Burnam (b. 1946), based on John 6
Music: *Kusik* Jack Warren Burnam (b. 1946)
© 1978 Jack Warren Burnam

Irr.

763 **As we gather at your table**

1. As we gath - er at your
2. Turn our wor - ship in - to

Ta - ble, as we lis - ten to your Word, help us
wit - ness in the sac - ra - ment of life; send us

know, O God, your pres - ence; let our hearts and minds be
forth to love and serve you, bring - ing peace where there is

stirred. Nour - ish us with sa - cred sto - ry till we
strife. Give us, Christ, your great com - pas - sion to for -

claim it as our own; teach us through this ho - ly
give as you for - gave; may we still be - hold your

ban - quet how to make Love's vic - t'ry known.
im - age in the world you died to save. *to verse 3*

Optional Descant

3. Gra - cious Spi - rit, help us

3. Gra - cious Spi - rit, help us

sum - mon oth - er guests to share that Feast where tri -

sum - mon oth - er guests to share that Feast where tri -

um - phant Love will wel - come those who had been last and

um - phant Love will wel - come those who had been last and

87.87. D

Taste and see

Taste and see. Taste and see the good - ness of the Lord. _____ O taste and see. Taste and see the good - ness of the Lord, _____ of the Lord.

Fine

1. I will bless the Lord at all times. _____
2. Glo - ri - fy the Lord with me. _____
3. Wor - ship the Lord all you peo - ple. _____

His praise shall al - ways be on my
To - geth - er let us all praise his
You'll want for noth - ing if you

lips; _____ my soul shall
name. _____ I called the
ask. _____ Taste and

glo - ry in the Lord; _____ for
Lord and he an - swered me; _____ from
see that God is good; _____ in

he has been so good to me. _____
all my trou - bles he set me free. _____
him we need put all our trust. _____

D.C.

Words: James E. Moore, Jr., para. of Psalm 34
Music: James E. Moore, Jr.

Irr.

O blessed spring

1. O bless-ed spring, where Word and sign em - brace us
2. Through sum - mer heat of youth - ful years, un - cer - tain
3. When au - tumn cools and youth is cold, when limbs their
4. As win - ter comes, as win - ters must, we breathe our
5. Christ, ho - ly Vine, Christ, liv - ing Tree, be praised for

in - to Christ the Vine: here Christ en - joins each one to
faith, re - bel - lious tears, sus - tained by Christ's in - fus - ing
heav - y har - vest hold, then through us, warm, the Christ will
last, re - turn to dust; still held in Christ, our souls take
this blest mys - ter - y: that Word and wa - ter thus re -

be a branch of this life - giv - ing Tree.
rain, the boughs will shout for joy _____ a - gain.
move with gifts of beau - ty, wis - dom, love.
wing and trust the prom - ise of _____ the spring.
vive and join us to your Tree _____ of Life.

Words: Susan Palo Cherwien (b. 1953); © 1993 Susan Palo Cherwien
Music: *Berglund*, Robert Buckley Farlee (b. 1950); © 1993 Robert Buckley Farlee

LM

You're called by name, forever loved 766

1. You're called by name, for - ev - er loved, a - dopt - ed as a child of God. Now one with us, the fam - i - ly of those who know and love the Lord.

2. Marked as Christ's own, signed by the cross where Je - sus for our sins once died. With Je - sus bur - ied in his death, called to con - fess Christ cru - ci - fied.

3. Raised to new life, a life of grace, set free from sin, in Christ to grow; his res - ur - rec - tion to pro - claim, his love in all of life to know.

4. Sealed by the Spi - rit, Lord of life, sus - tained and strength - ened by his might. Joined to the church to share, with us, the in - her - i - tance of saints in light.

Refrain

Lord, in your hands we place your own. Lord,

In your hands we place your own. Lord,

Lord, in your hands we place your own. Lord,

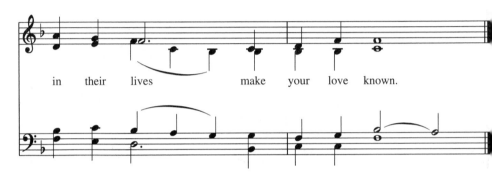

in their lives make your love known.

Words: Rosalind Brown (b. 1953);
Music: *Sara H.*, Kevin R. Hackett (b. 1956)

767   Baptized in water

1. Bap - tized in wa - ter, sealed by the Spi - rit, cleansed by the
2. Bap - tized in wa - ter, sealed by the Spi - rit, dead in the
3. Bap - tized in wa - ter, sealed by the Spi - rit, marked with the

blood	of	Christ	our King:	heirs	of sal - va - tion,
tomb	with	Christ	our King:	one	with his ris - ing.
sign	of	Christ	our King:	born	of one Fa - ther,

trust - ing	his prom - ise,	faith - ful - ly now	God's praise we sing.
freed and	for - giv - en,	thank - ful - ly now	God's praise we sing.
we are	his child - ren,	joy - ful - ly now	God's praise we sing.

Words: Michael Saward (b. 1932); © 1982 Hope Publishing Co., Carol Stream,
Il, 60188. All rights reserved. Used by permission.
Music: Eugene W. Hancock (1929-1994); © 1992 Eugene W. Hancock
You must contact Hope Publishing Co. to reproduce these words.

55.85.58

I believe in God almighty 768

1. I be - lieve in God al - might - y, Au - thor of all things that
2. I be - lieve that Je - sus suf - fered, scourged and scorned and cru - ci -
3. I be - lieve in God's own Spir - it, bond - ing all the saints with-

be, Mak - er of the earth and heav-ens, Keep - er of the sky and
fied; tak - en from the cross, was bur - ied— True Life there had tru - ly
in one church, cath - o - lic and ho - ly, where for - give - ness frees from

sea. I be - lieve in God's Son, Je - sus, now for
died. I be - lieve that on the third day Christ was
sin; in the bod - y's res - ur - rec - tion, for the

us both Lord and Christ, of the Spir - it and of
raised up from the grave, then as - cend - ed to God's
break - ing of death's chain gives the life that's ev - er -

Mar - y born to bring a - bun - dant life.
right hand. He will come to judge and save.
last - ing. This the faith that I have claimed.

Words: Sylvia G. Dunstan (1955-1993); © 1991 GIA Publications, Inc.
Music: *Domhnach Trionoide*, Gaelic melody; © 1991 GIA Publications, Inc.
    harm. Richard Proulx (b. 1937) © 1975 GIA Publications, Inc.
    You must contact GIA Publications, Inc. to reproduce this selection.   87.87.D

1. I be - lieve in God al - might - y, Au - thor of all
2. I be - lieve that Je - sus suf - fered, scourged and scorned and
3. I be - lieve in God's own Spir - it, bond - ing all the

things that be, Mak - er of the earth and heav - ens,
cru - ci - fied; tak - en from the cross, was bur - ied—
saints with - in one church, cath - o - lic and ho - ly,

Keep - er of the sky and sea. I be - lieve in
True Life there had tru - ly died. I be - lieve that
where for - give - ness frees from sin; in the bod - y's

God's Son, Je - sus, now for us both Lord and Christ of the Spir - it
on the third day Christ was raised up from the grave, then as - cend - ed
res - ur - rec - tion, for the break - ing of death's chain gives the life that's

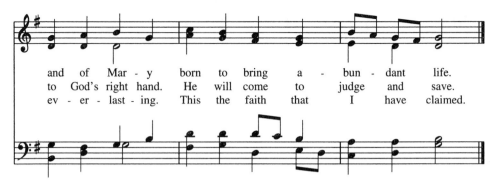

and of Mar - y born to bring a - bun - dant life.
to God's right hand. He will come to judge and save.
ev - er - last - ing. This the faith that I have claimed.

Words: Sylvia G. Dunstan (1955-1993); © 1991 GIA Publications, Inc.
Music: *Arfon* (Major), Welsh hymn melody, harm. Carlton R. Young, alt.
arr. © 1964 Abingdon Press
You must contact GIA Publications, Inc. to reproduce these words.

87.87.D

770   O God of gentle strength

1. O God of gen - tle strength, your love em -
2. Your wa - ters of re - birth have claimed us
3. And when life's chal - len - ges e - clipse our
4. Where will the jour - ney lead? The path may

bra - ces me. With - in the sure - ness of your care
as your own. As mem - bers of one bod - y, we
minds with doubt, let ho - ly wis - dom spark a flame
be ob - scure. But prom - ised hope of things un - seen

my heart rests will - ing - ly.
shall nev - er be a - lone.
to drive the dark - ness out.
will keep our foot - ing sure.

Words: Patricia B. Clark (b. 1938); © Patricia B. Clark.
Music: *Shoshana*, Jane Manton Marshall (b. 1924); © 1994 by Hope Publishing Co., Carol Stream, IL 60188.
  All rights reserved. Used by permission. *You must contact Hope Publishing Co., Inc. to reproduce this music.*

SM

O God of gentle strength

771

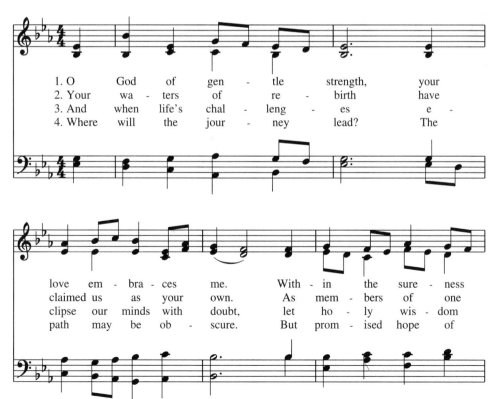

1. O God of gen - tle strength, your
2. Your wa - ters of re - birth have
3. And when life's chal - leng - es e -
4. Where will the jour - ney lead? The

love em - bra - ces me. With - in the sure - ness
claimed us as your own. As mem - bers of one
clipse our minds with doubt, let ho - ly wis - dom
path may be ob - scure. But prom - ised hope of

of your care my heart rests will - ing - ly.
bod - y, we shall nev - er be a - lone.
spark a flame to drive the dark - ness out.
things un - seen will keep our foot - ing sure.

Words: Patricia B. Clark (b. 1938); © 1995 Patricia B. Clark
Music: *Carlisle*, Charles Lockhart (1745-1815)

SM

772 O Christ, the healer

1. O Christ, the heal - er, we have come to pray for
2. From ev - ery ail - ment flesh en - dures our bod - ies
3. How strong, O Lord, are our de - sires, how weak our
4. In con - flicts that de - stroy our health we rec - og -
5. Grant that we all, made in one faith, in your com -

health, to plead for friends. How can we fail to
clam - or to be freed; yet in our hearts we
know - ledge of our-selves! Re - lease in us those
nize the world's dis - ease; our com - mon life de -
mu - ni - ty may find the whole-ness that, en -

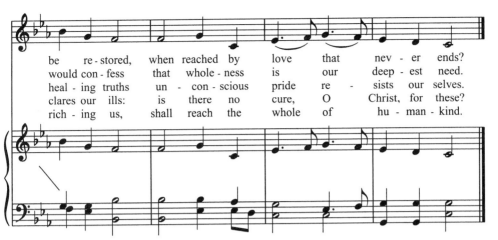

be re-stored, when reached by love that nev-er ends?
would con-fess that whole-ness is our deep-est need.
heal-ing truths un - con-scious pride re - sists our selves.
clares our ills: is there no cure, O Christ, for these?
rich-ing us, shall reach the whole of hu-man-kind.

Heal me, hands of Jesus   773

1. Heal me, hands of Je-sus, and search out all my pain: re-
2. Cleanse me, blood of Je-sus, take bit-ter-ness a - way; let
3. Know me, mind of Je-sus, and show me all my sin; dis-
4. Fill me, joy of Je-sus: anx-i - e - ty shall cease and

store my hope, re-move my fear and bring me peace a - gain.
me for-give as one for-given and bring me peace to - day.
pel the mem-o - ries of guilt, and bring me peace with - in.
heaven's se - ren-i - ty be mine, for Je - sus brings me peace!

774 From miles around the sick ones came

1. From miles a-round the sick ones came, in hope that One they
2. And still they come, new preys of plague, while of-ten in their
3. Re-call us to our mis-sion, Lord, to reach for those cut

heard was Lord would make their souls and bod-ies
rooms of prayer God's peo-ple wor-ship, safe and
off, in pain; to of-fer friend-ship, strength, and

[1. 2.]

well, with heal-ing touch or sav - ing word.
sound, un-heed-ing, e-ven un - a - ware.
peace and be a faith-ful church a - **[1. 2.]**

[3.]

3. gain. **[3.]**

Words: Jane Manton Marshall (b. 1924); © 1994 by Hope Publishing Co., Carol Stream, IL 60188.
    All rights reserved. Used by permission.
Music: *Tucker*, David Ashley White (b. 1944); © 1994 Selah Publishing Co. Inc.
    You must contact Hope Publishing Co. to reproduce the words and Selah Publishing Co., Inc. to reproduce the music.

LM

Give thanks for life

1. Give thanks for life, the meas-ure of our days,
2. Give thanks for those who made their life a light
3. And for our own, our liv-ing and our dead,
4. Give thanks for hope, that like the wheat, the grain

mor-tal, we pass through beau-ty that de-cays, yet
caught from the Christ flame burst-ing through the night, who
thanks for the love by which our life is fed, a
ly-ing in dark-ness does its life re-tain, in

sing to God our hope, our love, our praise,
touched the truth, who burned for what is right,
love not changed by time or death or dread,
res-ur-rec-tion to grow green a-gain.

Al -

le - lu - ia, Al - le - lu - ia!

10 10 10 with Alleluias

776   No saint on earth lives life to self alone

1. No   saint   on   earth lives life   to   self   a - lone
2. For   to   this   end   our   Lord by   death was   slain,

or   dies   a - lone, for   we   with Christ are   one.
that   to   new   life   he   might a - rise   a - gain.

So   if   we   live,   for Christ a - lone   we   live,
Through sor - row on   to   tri - umph Christ has   led,

and if we die, to Christ our dy - ing give.
and reigns o'er all: the liv - ing and the dead.

In liv - ing and in dy - ing this con - fess:
In liv - ing and in dy - ing, him we bless.

we are the Lord's, safe in God's faith - ful - ness.
We are the Lord's, safe in God's faith - ful - ness.

Words: J. W. Schulte-Nordholt; tr. Norman J. Kansfield; © Norman J. Kansfield
Music: *Song 1*, melody and bass Orlando Gibbons (1583-1625); harm. Ralph Vaughn Williams
(1872-1958), alt., from *Hymns for Church and School* 1964; harm. © Oxford University Press   10 10.10 10.10 10

Sing alleluia forth in duteous praise   777

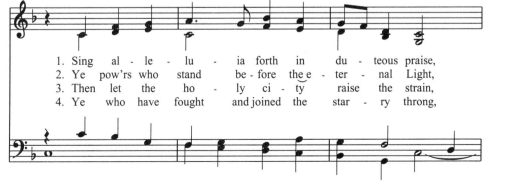

1. Sing al - le - lu - ia forth in du - teous praise,
2. Ye pow'rs who stand be - fore the e - ter - nal Light,
3. Then let the ho - ly ci - ty raise the strain,
4. Ye who have fought and joined the star - ry throng,

ye ci - ti - zens of heav'n, O sweet - ly raise an end - less
let all your choirs re - ech - o to the height an end - less
and with glad songs re - sound - ing wake a - gain an end - less
ye vic - tors, now take up the e - ter - nal song, an end - less

al - le - lu - ia.

5. Your songs of triumph shall forever ring
   the hymns which tell the honor of your King,
   an endless alleluia.

6. Such song is rest and food and deep delight
   to saints forgiven; let them all unite
   in endless alleluia.

7. Almighty Christ, to thee our voices sing
   all laud forevermore; to thee we bring
   an endless alleluia.

Words: Latin, 5th-8th cent.; ver. *Hymnal 1940*, Tr. © 1941, 1943, 1961, 1981
Church Pension Fund
Music: *Piepkorn*, Robert Buckley Farlee (b. 1950); © 1995 Robert Buckley Farlee

10.10.7

778   **We all are one in mission**

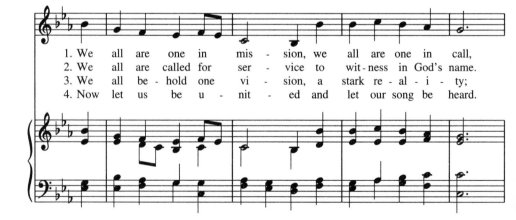

1. We all are one in mis - sion, we all are one in call,
2. We all are called for ser - vice to wit - ness in God's name.
3. We all be - hold one vi - sion, a stark re - al - i - ty;
4. Now let us be u - nit - ed and let our song be heard.

our var - ied gifts u - nit - ed by Christ, the Lord of all.
Our min - is - tries are dif - f'rent, our pur - pose is the same:
the stew - ard of sal - va - tion was nailed up - on a tree.
Now let us be a ves - sel for God's re - deem - ing Word.

A sin - gle, great com - mis - sion com - pels us from a - bove
to touch the lives of oth - ers by God's sur - pris - ing grace,
Yet res - ur - rect - ed Jus - tice gives rise that we may share
We all are one in mis - sion, we all are one in call,

to plan and work to - geth - er that all may know Christ's love.
so peo - ple of all na - tions may feel God's warm em - brace.
free re - con - cil - i - a - tion and hope a - mid de - spair.
our var - ied gifts u - nit - ed by Christ, the Lord of all.

779　The church of Christ in every age

1. The church of Christ in ev - ery age, be - set by
2. A - cross the world, a - cross the street, the vic - tims
3. Then let the ser - vant church a - rise. A car - ing
4. For Christ a - lone, whose blood was shed, can cure the
5. We have no mis - sion but to serve in full o -

change but spir - it led, must claim and test its her - i -
of in - jus - tice cry for shel - ter and for bread to
church that longs to be a part - ner in Christ's sac - ri -
fe - ver in our blood. And teach us how to share our
be - dience to our Lord: to care for all with - out re -

tage and keep on ri - sing from the dead.
eat and nev - er live un - til they die.
fice, and clothed in Christ's hu - man - i - ty.
bread and feed the starv - ing mul - ti - tude.
serve. And spread Christ's lib - er - a - ting word.

Words: Fred Pratt Green (b. 1903); © 1971 Hope Publishing Co., Carol Stream, IL 60188.
All rights reserved. Used by permission.
Music: *Dunedin*, Vernon Griffiths (1894-1985); reprinted from the *New Catholic Hymnal*
© Copyright by Faber Music Ltd. Used by permission of Boosey and Hawkes, Inc., Sole Agent
You must contact Hope Publishing Co. to reproduce these words.

LM

Lord, you give the great commission 780

1. Lord, you give the great com - mis - sion: "Heal the
2. Lord, you call us to your ser - vice: "In my
3. Lord, you make the com - mon ho - ly: "This my
4. Lord, you show us love's true mea - sure: "Fa - ther,
5. Lord, you bless with words as - sur - ing: "I am

sick and preach the word." Lest the church ne -
name bap - tize and teach." That the world may
bod - y, this my blood." Let us all, for
what they do, for - give." Yet we hoard as
with you to the end." Faith and hope and

glect its mis - sion, and the gos - pel go un -
trust your prom - ise, life a - bun - dant meant for
earth's true glo - ry, dai - ly lift life heav - en -
pri - vate trea - sure all that you so free - ly
love re - stor - ing, may we serve as you in -

heard, help us wit - ness to your pur - pose
each, give us all new fer - vor, draw us
ward, ask - ing that the world a - round us
give. May your care and mer - cy lead us
tend and, a - mid the cares that claim us,

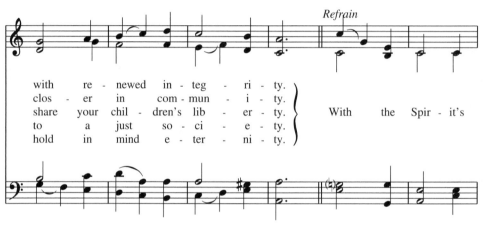

Refrain

with re - newed in - teg - ri - ty.
clos - er in com - mun - i - ty.
share your chil - dren's lib - er - ty.
to a just so - ci - e - ty.
hold in mind e - ter - ni - ty.

With the Spir - it's

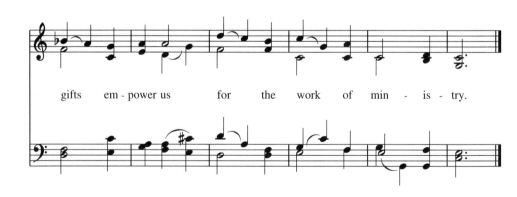

gifts em - power us for the work of min - is - try.

Words: Jeffery Rowthorn (b. 1934); © 1978 Hope Publishing Co.
Music: *Abbot's Leigh*, Cyril Vincent Taylor (1907-1991); © 1942.
    Renewal 1970, Hope Publishing Co., Carol Stream, IL 60188.
    All rights reserved. Used by permission.
    You must contact Hope Publishing Co. to reproduce this selection.

87.87D

Now let us rise and hymn the grace

1. Now let us rise and hymn the grace ____ that brings us
2. That we may o - pen love's em - brace ____ to wel - come
3. Re - joic - ing let us take this "Peace!" ____ In - to the

to this time and place. ____ Full ded - i - ca - tion
all the hu - man race, ____ here let no walls of
world that we in - crease ____ Christ's reign of jus - tice,

here is owed ____ the rich - es that our past be - stowed: ____ God, in this
hate di - vide, ____ but let Christ's "Peace!" a - lone a - bide. ____ God, help us
truth, and love ____ that heav - en come on earth, and of ____ this bless - ing

time your church re - new; ____ en - a - ble us your will ____ to do.
all this dream ful - fill; ____ en - a - ble us to do ____ your will.
we, with grace a - new, ____ still seek God's will to know ____ and do.

Words: John L. Hooker (b. 1944)
Music: *Owen*, John L. Hooker (b. 1944)
© 1993 John L. Hooker

88.88.88

782 Gracious Spirit, give your servants

1. Gra - cious Spir - it, give your ser - vants joy to set sin's
2. Word made flesh, who gave up glo - ry to be - come our
3. Lov - ing God, who birthed cre - a - tion from the noth - ing-
4. Tri - une God, e - ter - nal Be - ing, nev - er end - ing,

cap - tives free, hope to heal the bro - ken - heart - ed,
great high priest, tak - ing on our hu - man na - ture
ness of space, kin - dling life where all was emp - ty,
un - be - gun, bound - less grace and per - fect jus - tice,

peace to share love's li - ber - ty. Through us bring your balm of
to re - deem the last and least: let your cour - age and com-
turn - ing cha - os in - to grace: when we feel con - fused and
right - eous and for - giv - ing One: so en - fold us in your

glad - ness to the wound - ed and op - pressed; help us claim and
pas - sion shape and guide our min - is - tries; as our Sav - ior
fruit - less, dawn up - on our rest - less night; give us faith's im-
mer - cy that our wills and yours u - nite; through us may the

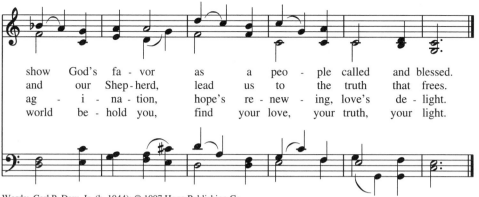

show God's fa - vor as a peo - ple called and blessed.
and our Shep - herd, lead us to the truth that frees.
ag - i - na - tion, hope's re - new - ing, love's de - light.
world be - hold you, find your love, your truth, your light.

Words: Carl P. Daw, Jr. (b. 1944); © 1997 Hope Publishing Co.
Music: *Abbot's Leigh,* Cyril Vincent Taylor (b. 1907);
© 1942. Renewal 1970 Hope Publishing Co., Carol Stream, IL 60188.
All rights reserved. Used by permission.
You must contact Hope Publishing Co. to reproduce this selection. 87.87.D

Heleluyan 783
Alleluia

He - le - lu - yan, he - le - lu - yan: he - le, he - le - lu - yan;
Al - le - lu - ia, al - le - lu - ia: al - le, al - le - lu - ia;

he - le - lu - yan, he - le - lu - yan: he - le, he - le - lu - yan.
al - le - lu - ia, al - le - lu - ia: al - le, al - le - lu - ia.

* May be sung as a round.

Setting: Muscogee (Creek) Indian, tr. Charles Webb
Transcription © 1989 by The United Methodist Publishing House.
Used by permission.

Hallelujah! We sing your praises! 784
Haleluya! Pelo tso rona

Hal - le - lu - jah! We sing your prais - es! All our
Ha - le - lu - ya! Pe - lo tsa ro - na, di tha -

hearts are filled with glad - ness! Hal - le - lu - jah! We sing your
bi - le ka - o - fe - la. Ha - le - lu - ya! Pe - lo tsa

Fine

prai - ses! All our hearts are filled with glad - ness!
ro - na, di tha - bi - le ka - o - fe - la.

Christ the Lord to us said: "I am wine, I am bread, I am
Je - sus says to us still: "All who do the Lord's will, all who

wine, I am bread, give to all who thirst and hun - ger!" **D.C.**
do the Lord's will are my sis - ters and my bro - thers." D.C.

Words: South African
Music: *Haleluya! Pelo tso rona*, South African © 1984 Utryck, admin. Walton Music Corporation

Irr.

785 Santo, santo, santo
Holy, holy, holy

San - to, san - to, san - to, mi cor - a - zon te a - do - ra! Mi
Ho - ly, ho - ly, ho - ly, my heart, my heart a - dores you! My

cor - a - zon te sa - be de - cir: san - to e - res Se - ñor.
heart is glad to say the words: you are ho - ly, Lord.

Words: Variation on a traditional liturgical text
Music: Composer of melody unknown; arr. © 1990 Iona Community, admin. by GIA Publications, Inc.
based on two-part version as taught by Pablo D. Sosa (b.1933)
You must contact GIA Publications, Inc. to reproduce this arrangement.

Irr.

Cantad al Señor

786

1. Can - tad al Se - ñor un cán - ti - co
2. El es cre - a - dor y due - ño de
3. Can - tad a Je - sús por - que el es
4. Es el quien nos dio su Es - pí - ri - tu
5. Can - tad al Se - ñor, "¡A - mén, a - le -

1. nue - vo, can - tad al Se - ñor un cán - ti - co
2. to - do, el es cre - a - dor y due - ño de
3. dig - no, can - tad a Je - sús por - que el es
4. San - to, es el quien nos dio su Es - pí - ri - tu
5. lu - ya!" Can - tad al Se - ñor, "¡A - mén, a - le -

1. nue - vo, can - tad al Se - ñor un cán - ti - co
2. to - do, el es cre - a - dor y due - ño de
3. dig - no, can - tad a Je - sús por - que el es
4. San - to, es el quien nos dio su Es - pí - ri - tu
5. lu - ya!" Can - tad al Se - ñor, "¡A - mén, a - le -

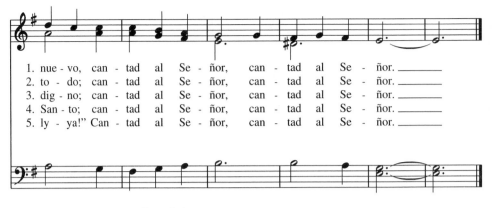

Translation

1. *Sing to the Lord a new song.*
2. *He is the creator and owner of all.*
3. *Sing to the Lord because he is almighty.*
4. *It is he who gave us his Holy Spirit.*
5. *Sing to the Lord, Amen! Alleluia!*

Words: Anonymous, Brazilian
Music: *Cantai ao Senhor*, Brazilian; arr. Felipe Blycker J.;
     harm. Samuel Pascoe © Samuel Pascoe

11.11.11.10

787   We are marching in the light of God
Siyahamb' ekukhanyen' kwenkhos'
Marcharemos en la luz de Dios

We are march-ing ___
Si - ya - ham - ba ___
Mar - cha - re - mos ___

light of God. We are march-ing, march-ing, we are
nyen' kwen - khos'. Si - ya - ham - be, ham - ba, si - ya -
luz de Dios. Mar - cha - re - mos, - re - mos mar - cha -

Oo ___
Oo ___
Oo ___

march-ing, march-ing we are march-ing in the light of God. ___
ham - ba, ham - ba, si - ya - hamb' e - ku - kha - nyen' kwen - khos'. ___
re - mos re - mos mar - cha - re - mos en la luz de Dios. ___

Words: South African; Spanish words, Bernardo Murray
Music: *Siyahamba*, South African © 1984 Utryck, admin.
    Walton Music Corporation

Irr.

788   As newborn stars were stirred to song

1. As new-born stars were stirred to song when all things came to
2. In psalms that raise the sing-er's sense to un-i-vers-al
3. When God's re-deem-ing Word took flesh to make sal-va-tion
4. But si-lence won no vic-t'ry there; a rest was all it

be, as Mir-i-am and Mos-es sang when
truths, in pro-phet's dark-toned o-ra-cle or
sure, un-heed-ing hearts at-tuned to strife re -
scored be-fore glad al-le-lu-ias rose to

Is-rael was set free, so mu-sic bursts un-bid-den
hymn of three brave youths: the song of faith and praise en -
fused love's o-ver-ture. Yet to the end the song went
greet the ris-en Lord. The church still keeps that song a -

forth   when   God - filled hearts re - joice,   to wak - en
dured   through those God called to   be   a cho - sen
on: a   sup - per's part - ing hymn,   a psalm in -
live,   for   death has lost its sting,   and with the

awe   and grat - i - tude and give mute faith   a
peo - ple bear - ing light for all the world   to
toned on dy - ing lips when sun and hope   grew
gift   of life re - newed the heart will ev - er

1, 2, 3.   **4.**

voice.
see.
dim.
       sing.

CMD

Peace among earth's peoples 789

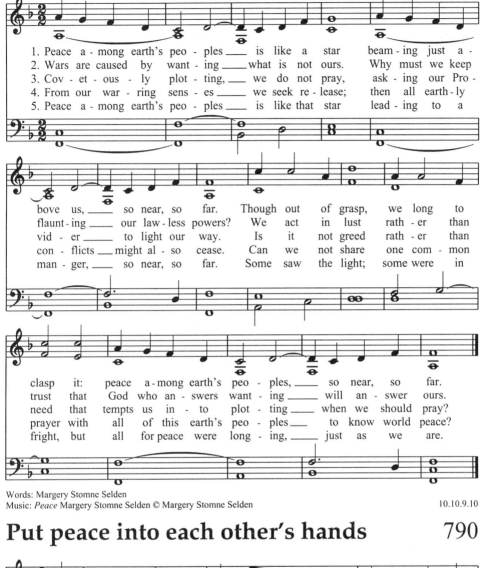

1. Peace a - mong earth's peo - ples ___ is like a star beam - ing just a -
2. Wars are caused by want - ing ___ what is not ours. Why must we keep
3. Cov - et - ous - ly plot - ting, ___ we do not pray, ask - ing our Pro -
4. From our war - ring sens - es ___ we seek re - lease; then all earth - ly
5. Peace a - mong earth's peo - ples ___ is like that star lead - ing to a

bove us, ___ so near, so far. Though out of grasp, we long to
flaunt - ing ___ our law - less powers? We act in lust rath - er than
vid - er ___ to light our way. Is it not greed rath - er than
con - flicts ___ might al - so cease. Can we not share one com - mon
man - ger, ___ so near, so far. Some saw the light; some were in

clasp it: peace a - mong earth's peo - ples, ___ so near, so far.
trust that God who an - swers want - ing ___ will an - swer ours.
need that tempts us in - to plot - ting ___ when we should pray?
prayer with all of this earth's peo - ples ___ to know world peace?
fright, but all for peace were long - ing, ___ just as we are.

Words: Margery Stomne Selden
Music: *Peace* Margery Stomne Selden © Margery Stomne Selden

10.10.9.10

Put peace into each other's hands 790

1. Put peace in - to each oth - er's hands and like a trea - sure
2. Put peace in - to each oth - er's hands with lov - ing ex - pec -
3. Put peace in - to each oth - er's hands, like bread we break for
4. As at com - mu - nion, shape your hands in - to a wait - ing
5. Put Christ in - to each oth - er's hands, he is love's deep - est

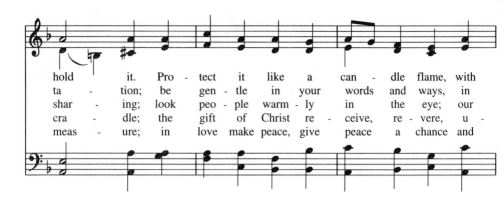

hold   it.   Pro - tect it like a can - dle flame, with
ta - tion; be gen - tle in your words and ways, in
shar - ing; look peo - ple warm - ly in the eye; our
cra - dle; the gift of Christ re - ceive, re - vere, u -
meas - ure; in love make peace, give peace a chance and

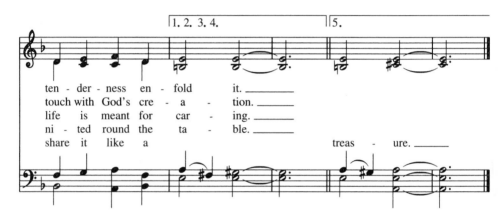

1. 2. 3. 4.   **5.**

ten - der - ness en - fold   it. _____
touch with God's cre - a -   tion. _____
life is meant for car -   ing. _____
ni - ted round the ta -   ble. _____
share it like a   treas - ure. _____

Words: Fred Kaan (b. 1929); © 1989 Hope Publishing Co., Carol Stream, IL 60188.
     All rights reserved. Used by permission.
Music: *Peta*, John L. Hooker (b. 1944); © 1989 John L. Hooker
     You must contact Hope Publishing Co. to reproduce these words.

87.87

791   Peace before us

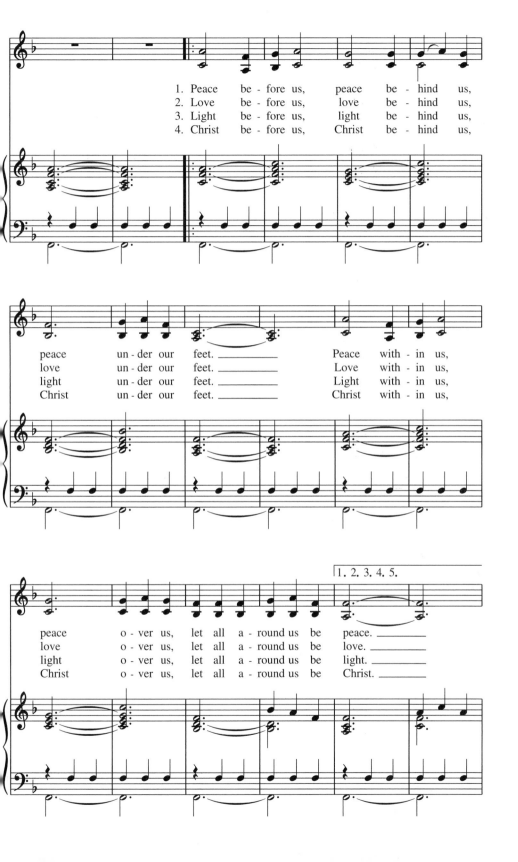

5. Alleluia, alleluia, alleluia.
   Alleluia, alleluia, alleluia.
6. Peace before us, peace behind us,
   peace under our feet.
   Peace within us, peace over us,
   let all around us be peace. *(three times)*

Words: David Haas (b. 1957), based on a Navaho prayer © 1987 GIA Publications, Inc.
Music: David Haas (b. 1957) © 1987, GIA Publications, Inc.
   You must contact GIA Publications, Inc. to reproduce this selection.   Irr.

Holy God, you raise up prophets

1. Ho - ly God, you raise up proph-ets; praise and hon-or do we sing,
2. Mo - ral con-science of his na - tion, re-con-cil-ing black and white,
3. Teach-er of Christ-like non - vio-lence to the out-cast, poor and meek;
4. Preach-er of Christ's love for neigh-bor, he won No-bel's prize for peace;

for your faith-ful, hum-ble ser - vant, Doc - tor Mar-tin Luth-er King.
dreamed he of a just so-cie - ty, we must car-ry on his fight.
great - er weap-on 'gainst op-pres - sion is to turn the o - ther cheek.
peo - ples, beat your swords to plough-shares, wars 'twixt na-tions all shall cease.

Refrain

Bless - ed Mar-tin, pas - tor, proph-et, you the moun-tain - top did see;

Bless - ed Mar-tin, ho - ly mar-tyr: pray that we may all be free.

5. Champion of oppressed humanity
    suff'ring throughout all the world;
  he offered pride and dignity
    let Christ's banner be unfurled!
      Refrain

6. So, when felled by sniper's bullet,
    under heavens overcast,
  he could cry, "Thank God Almighty,
    I am free, I'm free at last!"
      Refrain

Words: Harold T. Lewis (b. 1947), © 1992 Harold T. Lewis
Music: *Martin's Song* by Carl Haywood (b. 1949), from *Songs of Praise*, © 1992 Carl Haywood
   You must contact Carl Haywood to reproduce this music.

Irr.

793   Here, O Lord, your servants gather
Sekai no tomo to te o tsunagi

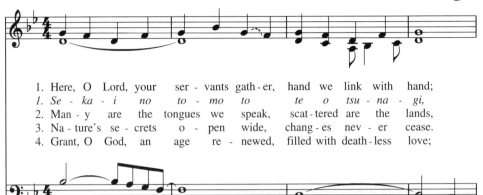

1. Here, O Lord, your ser - vants gath-er, hand we link with hand;
1. *Se - ka - i no to - mo to te o tsu - na - gi,*
2. Man - y are the tongues we speak, scat - tered are the lands,
3. Na - ture's se - crets o - pen wide, chang - es nev - er cease.
4. Grant, O God, an age re - newed, filled with death - less love;

look - ing toward our Sav - ior's cross, joined in love we stand.
Jyu - ji - ka no mo - to ni ta - tsu wa - re - ra,
yet our hearts are one in God, one in love's de - mands.
Where, oh where, can wea - ry souls find the source of peace?
help us as we work and pray, send us from a - bove

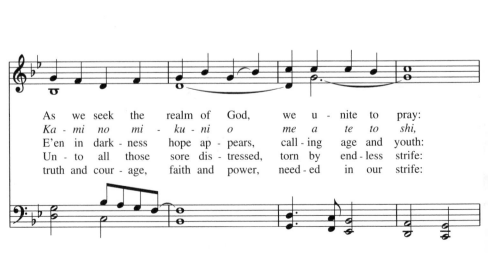

As we seek the realm of God, we u - nite to pray:
Ka - mi no mi - ku - ni o me a te to shi,
E'en in dark - ness hope ap - pears, call - ing age and youth:
Un - to all those sore dis - tressed, torn by end - less strife:
truth and cour - age, faith and power, need - ed in our strife:

Je - sus, Sav - ior, guide our steps, for you are the Way.
Shu Ye - su no mi - chi o su - su - mi yu - kan.
Je - sus, teach - er, dwell with us, for you are the Truth.
Je - sus, heal - er, bring your balm, for you are the Life.
Je - sus, Mas - ter, be our Way, be our Truth, our Life.

Words: Tokuo Yamaguchi (b. 20th c.); trans. Everett M. Stowe (b. 20th c.); © 1958 The United
Methodist Publishing House; phonetic transcription from the Japanese by I-to Loh (b. 1936);
© 1989 The United Methodist Publishing House
Music: Isao Koizumi (b. 1907); © 1958 by Isao Koizumi, Used by permisiion of JASRAC,   75.75D
License No. 971288-701. *You must contact JASRAC to reproduce this music.*

Muchos resplandores   794
Many are the light beams

1. Mu - chos res-plan-do - res, só - lo u - na luz; es la
2. Mu - chas son las ra - mas, un ár - bol hay, y su
1. Man - y are the light - beams from the one light. Our one
2. Man - y are the bran - ches of the one tree. Our one

luz de Cris - to. _____ Mu - chos res-plan-do - res,
tron - co es Cris - to. _____ Mu - chos son los tron - cos,
light is Je - sus. _____ Man - y are the light - beams
tree is Je - sus. _____ Man - y are the bran - ches

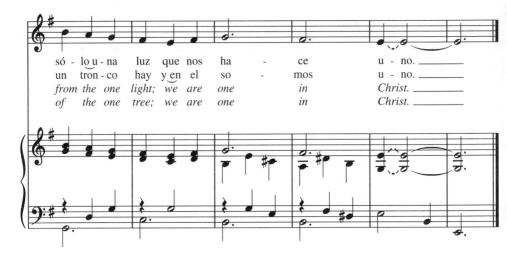

só - lo u - na luz que nos ha - ce u - no. _____
un tron - co hay y en el so - mos u - no. _____
from the one light; we are one in Christ. _____
of the one tree; we are one in Christ. _____

3. Muchos son los dones, uno el amor:
   el amor de Cristo.
   Muchos son los dones, uno el amor
   que nos hace uno.

4. Muchas las tareas, uno el sentir,
   el sentir de Cristo.
   Muchas las tareas, uno el sentir
   que nos hace uno.

5. Muchos son los miembros, un cuerpo hay,
   ese cuerpo es Cristo.
   Muchos son los miembros, un cuerpo hay
   y en El somos uno.

3. *Many are the gifts giv'n, love is all one.*
   Love's the gift of Jesus.
   Many are the gifts giv'n, love is all one;
   we are one in Christ.

4. *Many ways to serve God, the spirit is one;*
   servant spirit of Jesus.
   Many ways to serve God, the spirit is one;
   we are one in Christ.

5. *Many are the members, the body is one;*
   members all of Jesus.
   Many are the members, the body is one;
   we are one in Christ.

Words: Anders Frostenson (b. 1905) © AF-Foundation Hymns and Song, Verbum Stockholm
tr. Pablo D. Sosa (b. 1933); tr. © Pablo D. Sosa
Music: *Tjänsterna*, Olle Widestrand, harm. © Olle Widestrand harm. Skinner Chávez Melo (1944-1992)
© harm. Skinner Chavez-Melo   Irr.

795   **Come now, O Prince of Peace**

1. Come now, O Prince of Peace, make us one bod - y,
2. Come now, O God of love, make us one bod - y,
3. Come now and set us free, O God, our Sav - ior,
4. Come, Hope of U - ni - ty, make us one bod - y,

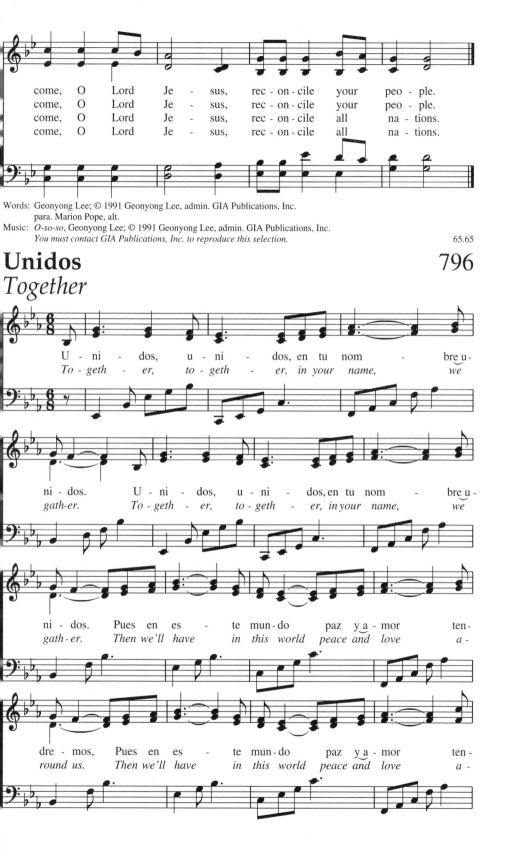

paz, _____ de a - mor y de paz. _____
peace, _____ *with love and peace.* _____

Words: Benjamin Villanueva, 1982; © 1983 Benjamin Villanueva;
tr. George Lockwood, 1983; © 1983 George Lockwood
Music: *Unidos,* Benjamin Villanueva, 1982; ©1983 Benjamin Villanueva; arr. Esther Frances, 1983, alt.

Irr.

It's me, it's me, it's me, O Lord 797

It's me, it's me, O Lord, Stand - in' in the need of prayer; __
It's me,

__ It's me, It's me, O Lord, Stand - in' in the need of prayer. __
It's me,

Fine

1. Not my broth - er, not my sis - ter, but it's me, O Lord,
2. Not the preach - er, not the dea - con, but it's me, O Lord,
3. Not my fa - ther, not my moth - er, but its me, O Lord,
4. Not the stran - ger, not my neigh - bor, but it's me, O Lord,

stand - in' in the need of prayer, not my broth - er, not my sis - ter, but it's
stand - in' in the need of prayer, not the preach - er, not the dea - con, but it's
stand - in' in the need of prayer, not my fa - ther, not my moth - er, but its
stand - in' in the need of prayer, not the stran - ger, not my neigh - bor, but it's

D.C.

me, O Lord, stand - in' in the need of prayer.
me, O Lord, stand - in' in the need of prayer.
me, O Lord, stand - in' in the need of prayer.
me, O Lord, stand - in' in the need of prayer.

Words: Traditional
Music: Negro Spiritual; arr. Carl Haywood (b. 1949), from *The Haywood Collection of Negro Spirituals*
  © 1992 Carl Haywood.
  You must contact Carl Haywood to reproduce this selection.   Irr.

798   Lord Jesus, think on me

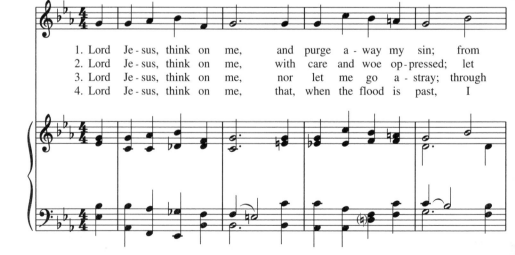

1. Lord Je - sus, think on me, and purge a - way my sin; from
2. Lord Je - sus, think on me, with care and woe op - pressed; let
3. Lord Je - sus, think on me, nor let me go a - stray; through
4. Lord Je - sus, think on me, that, when the flood is past, I

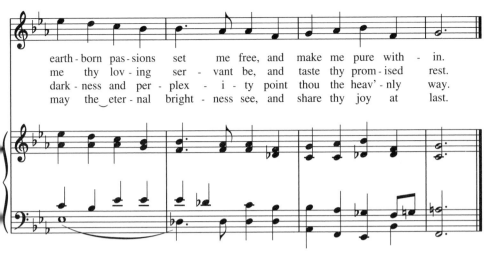

earth - born pas - sions set me free, and make me pure with - in.
me thy lov - ing ser - vant be, and taste thy prom - ised rest.
dark - ness and per - plex - i - ty point thou the heav' - nly way.
may the eter - nal bright - ness see, and share thy joy at last.

Words: Synesius of Cyrene (375?414?); tr. Allen William Chatfield (1808-1896), alt.
Music: *Barnfield*, Joseph Barnby, (1838-1896); harm. Owen Burdick (b. 1954); harm.
        © 1981 Owen Burdick

SM

Abide with me: fast falls the eventide   799

1. A - bide with me: fast falls the e - ven - tide;
2. I need thy pre - sence ev - 'ry pass - ing hour;
3. I fear no foe, with thee at hand to bless;
4. Hold thou thy cross be - fore my clos - ing eyes;

the dark - ness deep - ens; Lord, with me a - bide:
what but thy grace can foil the tempt - er's power?
ills have no weight, and tears no bit - ter - ness.
shine through the gloom, and point me to the skies;

when   oth - er   help - ers   fail   and   com - forts flee,
Who,   like thy - self,   my   guide and   stay   can be?
Where   is death's sting? Where, grave, thy   vic - to - ry?
heaven's morn - ing breaks, and earth's vain   sha - dows flee;

help   of   the   help - less, O   a - bide with me.
Through cloud and   sun - shine, Lord, a - bide with me.
I   tri - umph still,   if   thou a - bide with me.
in   life,   in   death, O Lord, a - bide with me.

Words: Henry F. Lyte, (1793-1847)
Music: *Dorland Mountain*, Randall Giles (b. 1950);
     © 1997 Randall Giles

10.10.10.10

800   Precious Lord, take my hand

1. Pre - cious Lord,   take my hand,   lead me   on,   let me
2. When my   way   grows drear,   pre - cious Lord,   lin - ger
3. When the dark - ness ap - pears and the night   draws

stand,   I am tired,   I am weak,   I am   worn; _____
near, when my life is   al - most gone; _____
near, and the day is   past and   gone; _____

through the storm, through the night, lead me on to the
hear my cry, hear my call, hold my hand, lest I
at the riv - er I stand, guide my feet, hold my

light, take my hand, pre-cious Lord, lead me on.____
fall, take my hand, pre-cious Lord, lead me on.____
hand, take my hand, pre-cious Lord, lead me on.____

Words: Thomas A. Dorsey (1899-1993)
Music: Thomas A. Dorsey; arr. Horace Clarence Boyer (b. 1935)

Irr.

God be with you till we meet again   801

Unison   *Harmony*

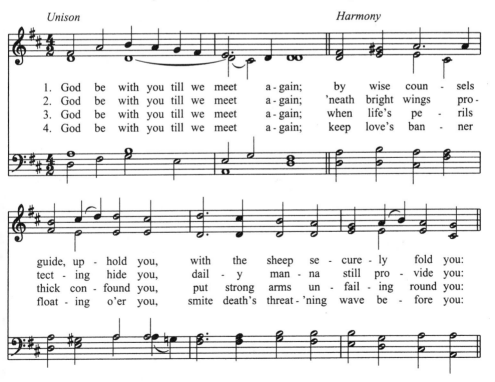

1. God be with you till we meet a - gain; by wise coun - sels
2. God be with you till we meet a - gain; 'neath bright wings pro -
3. God be with you till we meet a - gain; when life's pe - rils
4. God be with you till we meet a - gain; keep love's ban - ner

guide, up - hold you, with the sheep se - cure - ly fold you:
tect - ing hide you, dail - y man - na still pro - vide you:
thick con - found you, put strong arms un - fail - ing round you:
float - ing o'er you, smite death's threat - 'ning wave be - fore you:

Unison

God be with you till we meet a - gain.
God be with you till we meet a - gain.
God be with you till we meet a - gain.
God be with you till we meet a - gain.

Words: Jeremiah Eames Rankin (1828-1904), alt. John L. Hooker (b. 1944)
Music: *Randolph,* Ralph Vaughan Williams (1872-1958), alt.;
© Oxford University Press

98.89

802 Cuando el pobre nada tiene
When the poor one who has nothing

1. Cuan-do el po - bre na - da tie - ne y aùn re - par - te, ____
2. Cuan - do al - guien su - fre y lo - gra su con - sue - lo, ____
1. When a poor one who has noth-ing shares with strang - ers, ____
2. When at last all those who suf - fer find their com - fort, ____

____ cuan - do al - guien pa - sa sed y a - gua nos
____ cuan - do es - pe - ra y no se can - sa de es - pe -
____ *When the thirst - y wa - ter give un - to us*
____ *When they hope though e - ven hope seems hope - less -*

da, cuan-do el dé - bil a su her - ma - no for - ta -
rar, cuan-do a - ma - mos, aun-que el o - dio nos ro -
all, When the crip - pled in their weak - ness strength-en
ness, When we love though hate at times seems all a -

Estribillo (Refrain)

3. Cuando crece la alegría y nos inunda,
   cuando dicen nuestros labios la verdad,
   cuando do a mamos el sentirde los sencillos, *Estribillo*

4. Cuando abunda el bien y llena los hogares,
   cuando alguien donde hay guerra pone paz,
   cuando "hermano" le llamamos al extraño, *Estribillo*

3. *When our joy fills up our cup to overflowing,*
   When our lips can speak no words other than true,
   When we know that love for simple things is better. Refrain

4. *When our homes are filled with goodness in abundance.*
   When we learn how to make peace instead of war.
   When each stranger that we meet is called a neighbor. Refrain

Words: J. A. Olivar and Miguel Manzano
Music: *El Camino*, © 1971 J. A. Olivar and Miguel Manzano and San Pablo Internacional - SSP.   12.11.12.11.11
   All rights reserved. Sole U.S. Agent: OCP Publications, 5536 NE Hassalo,
   Portland, OR 97213. Used with permission.
   arr. Alvin Schutmaat
   You must contact OCP Publications to reproduce this selection.

These three are the treasures

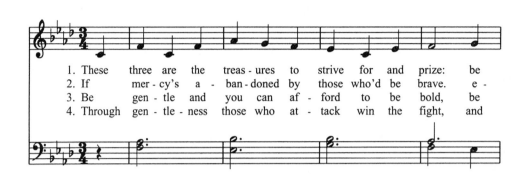

1. These three are the treas - ures to strive for and prize: be
2. If mer - cy's a - ban - doned by those who'd be brave. e -
3. Be gen - tle and you can af - ford to be bold, be
4. Through gen - tle - ness those who at - tack win the fight, and

gen - tle, live sim - ply and have the hum - il - it - y to shy from the
con - o - my squan - dered by those who'd be gen - er - ous, hu - mil - i - ty
fru - gal and so have e - nough to be lib - er - al, be hum - ble and
those who de - fend have their safe - ty in gen - tle - ness; this gen - tle - ness

strugg - le to put ones - self first, these are the pearls.
slight - ed by those who would lead, this is sure death.
thus be a lead - er of all, this is the way.
rests in the chil - dren of God, this is their sign.

Words: Colin Hodgetts
Music: *Song of Lau Tsu*, Colin Hodgetts © 1983 Stainer and Bell Ltd., All Rights Reserved. Used by permission of
Hope Publishing Company, Carol Stream, IL 60188.
You must contact Hope Publishing Co. to reproduce this selection.

11.13.11.4

Steal away

804

Steal a-way, steal a-way, steal a-way to Je-sus!

Fine

Steal a-way, steal a-way home, I ain't got long to stay here!

1. My Lord he calls me, he calls me by the thun-der. The
2. Green trees are bend-ing, poor sin-ner stands a-trem-bling, the
3. Tomb stones are burst-ing, poor sin-ner stands a-trem-bling, the
4. My Lord he calls me, he calls me by the light-ning. The

D.C.

trum-pet sounds with-in a my soul. I ain't got long to stay here.

Words: Traditional
Music: Negro Spiritual; arr. Carl Haywood (b. 1949), from *The Haywood Collections of Negro Spirituals.*
© 1992 Carl Haywood
You must contact Carl Haywood to reproduce this selection.

Irr.

I want Jesus to walk with me

Words: Traditional
Music: Negro Spiritual; arr. Carl Haywood (b. 1949), from *The Haywood Collection of Negro Spirituals.*
© 1992 Carl Haywood
You must contact Carl Haywood to reproduce this selection.

Irr.

If you believe and I believe 806

If you be-lieve and I be-lieve and we to-geth-er

pray, the Ho-ly Spir-it must come down and set God's peo-ple

free, and set God's peo-ple free, and set God's peo-ple

free; the Ho-ly Spir-it must come down and set God's peo-ple free.

Words: Traditional, Zimbabwe; adap. from English source as taught by Tarasai, ed. and
     arr. by John Bell © 1990 Iona Community/Wild Goose Publications, admin. GIA Publications, Inc.
Music: Traditional, Zimbabwe; adap. from English source as taught by Tarasai, ed. and
     arr. by John Bell © 1990 Iona Community/Wild Goose Publications, admin. GIA Publications, Inc.

You must contact GIA Publications, Inc. to reproduce this selection.   86.86.66.86

807   Put down your nets and follow me

1. "Put down your nets and fol - low me," our
2. We too are called from our con - cerns to
3. Do not be temp - ted by the cares of
4. The phan - tom rich - es we pur - sue are
5. "Put down your nets and fol - low me," our

1. Lord and Mas - ter said; and so they fol - lowed,
2. fol - low our Lord's way. By trust - ing him, the
3. long de - lud - ed dreams; temp - ta - tion's path is
4. nev - er ours to gain. They fade be - fore our
5. Lord and Mas - ter pleads; O may we fol - low

1. will - ing - ly, not know - ing where he led.
2. heart soon learns to cast off yes - ter - day.
3. wrought with snares and ne - ver as it seems.
4. eyes like dew af - ter a morn - ing rain.
5. faith - ful - ly, well know - ing where he leads.

Words: Janine Applegate (b. 1948); © 1997 Janine Applegate
Music: *Dillow*, Randall Giles (b. 1950); © 1997 Randall Giles

CM

Thuma mina

Send me, Lord

Additional verses

3. *Call:* Lead me, Lord, *Response:* Lead me, Jesus.
4. *Call:* Fill me, Lord, *Response:* Fill me, Jesus.

Words: South African
Music: *Thuma mina*, South African © 1984 Utryck, admin. Walton Music Corporation

Irr.

We adore you

Lord we love you, and we've come to rev-erence your ho-ly name. You are King of kings, You are Lord of lords, and we've come to wor-ship you with hearts of joy.

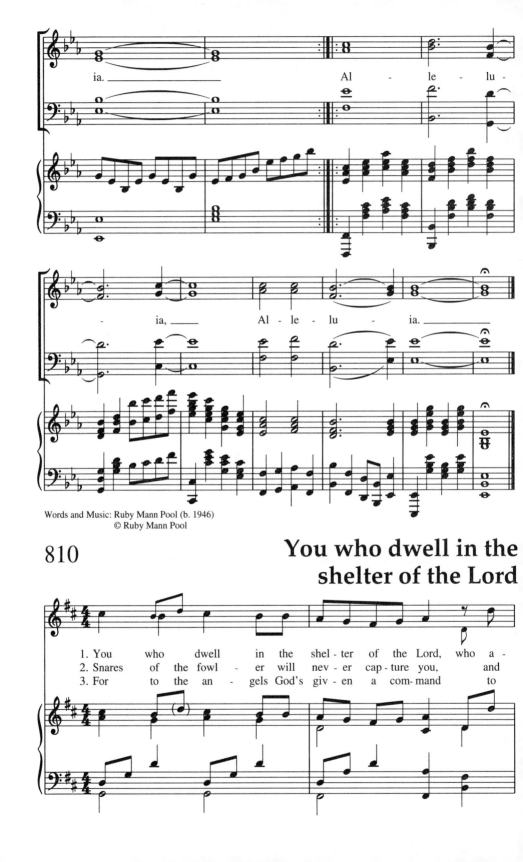

ia. _____ Al - le - lu -

- ia, _____ Al - le - lu - ia. _____

Words and Music: Ruby Mann Pool (b. 1946)
© Ruby Mann Pool

810

You who dwell in the shelter of the Lord

1. You who dwell in the shel-ter of the Lord, who a-
2. Snares of the fowl - er will nev - er cap-ture you, and
3. For to the an - gels God's giv-en a com-mand to

bide in this shad-ow for life,
fam-ine will bring you no fear;
guard you in all of your ways;

say to the Lord: "My
un-der God's wings your
up-on their hands they will

ref-uge, my rock in whom I trust!"
ref-uge with faith-ful-ness your shield.
bear you up, lest you dash your foot a-gainst a stone.

Refrain

"And I will raise you up on ea - gle's wings,

bear you on the breath of dawn, make you to shine like the

sun, and hold you in the palm of my hand."

Words and Music: Michael Joncas (b. 1951)
© 1979, 1991 New Dawn Music, 5536 NE Hassalo, Portland, OR 97213.
All rights reserved. Used by permission.
You must contact the copyright holder to reprint this selection.

811   You shall cross the barren desert

Verse 1

1. You shall cross the bar-ren des-ert, but you shall not die of thirst. You shall wan-der far in

safe-ty though you do not know the way. You shall
speak your words in for-eign lands and all will un-der-stand.
You shall see the face of God and live. _____

Refrain

Be not a-fraid. I go be-fore you al-ways.

Come, fol-low me, and I will give you rest. _____

Verse 2

2. If you pass through rag-ing wa-ters in the sea, you shall not drown, If you walk a-mid the burn-ing flames, you shall not be

harmed. If you stand be-fore the pow'r of hell and

death is at your side, know that I am with you _____ through it

To refrain   Verse 3

all. _____ 3. Bless-ed are your poor, for the

To refrain

rit.

king-dom shall be theirs. Blest are you that

Come fol-low me. and I will give you rest.

Words and Music: Bob Dufford, SJ

I, the Lord of sea and sky 812

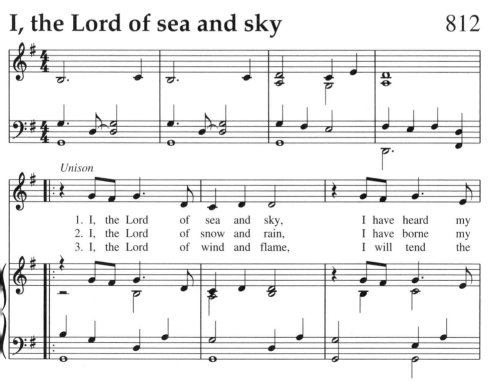

Unison

1. I, the Lord of sea and sky, I have heard my
2. I, the Lord of snow and rain, I have borne my
3. I, the Lord of wind and flame, I will tend the

Refrain

Here I am, Lord. ____ Is it I, Lord? ____ I have heard you call-ing in the night. ____ I will go, Lord, ____ if you lead me, ____ I will hold your peo - ple in my

1. 2. heart. ____

3. heart. ____

Words: Daniel L. Schutte
Music: Daniel L. Schutte
© 1981, Daniel L. Schutte; and New Dawn Music, 5536 NE Hassalo, Portland, OR 97213.
All rights reserved. Used by permission.
You must contact the copyright holder to reproduce this selection.

813

Way, way, way

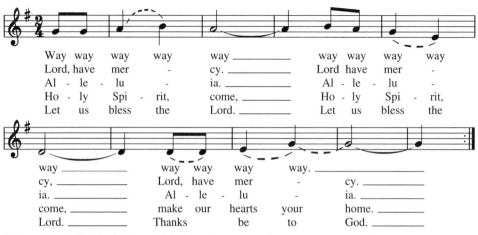

Way way way way way _____ way way way way

Lord, have mer - cy. _____ Lord have mer -

Al - le - lu - ia. _____ Al - le - lu -

Ho - ly Spi - rit, come, _____ Ho - ly Spi - rit,

Let us bless the Lord. _____ Let us bless the

way _____ way way way way. _____

cy, _____ Lord, have mer - cy. _____

ia. _____ Al - le - lu - ia. _____

come, _____ make our hearts your home. _____

Lord. _____ Thanks be to God. _____

Words and Music: Traditional Ojibway lullaby from *Chippewa Music* by Frances Densmore (1867-1957)
Each alternative text is sung independently and repeated numerous times.

814

Jesus Christ, Son of God

Je - sus Christ, Son of God, make your - self known through me.

Words and Music: Kevin R. Hackett (b. 1956)

815   Jesus said: The first commandment is this

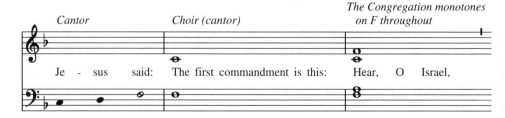

Cantor   *Choir (cantor)*   *The Congregation monotones on F throughout*

Je - sus said: The first commandment is this: Hear, O Israel,

The Lord our God is the on - ly Lord. Love the Lord your God with all your heart,

with all your soul, with all your mind, and with all your strength.

Choir (cantor)   *All*

The second is this: Love your neighbor as your - self.

There is no other com - mand - ment greater than these."

Setting: *Audi, Israel* Charles Rus (b. 1960)
©1990 Charles Rus

Christis risen from the dead   816

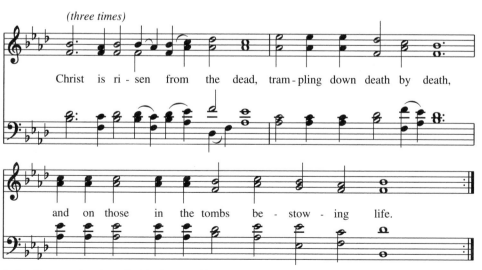

(three times)

Christ is ri - sen from the dead, tram - pling down death by death,

and on those in the tombs be - stow - ing life.

Setting: Znamenny chant; harm. Boris Ledkovsky (1894-1975)
© St. Vladimir Seminary Press

817   Christ is risen from the dead

(three times)

Christ is ri - sen from the dead, tramp - ling down death by death and on those in the tombs be - stow - ing life, _____ be - stow - ing life!

Setting: Early American, adapt. Richard Fabian (b. 1942)

818   Sh'ma Yisrael
Hear, O Israel

Sh'ma Yis - ra - el, A - do - nai El - o - hei - nu, A - do - nai e - chod. Ba - ruch shem ch' - vod, ch' - vod mal - chu - to l' - o - lam va - ed.

Hear, O Israel: The Lord our God, the Lord is One.
Praised be his name whose glorious kingdom is forever and ever.

Setting: Traditional Hebrew

Guide my feet Lord

1. Guide my feet Lord, while I run this race.
2. Hold my hand Lord, while I run this race.
3. Stand by me Lord, while I run this race.

Guide my feet Lord, while I run this race.
Hold my hand Lord, while I run this race.
Stand by me Lord, while I run this race.

Guide my feet Lord, while I run this race, 'cause I
Hold my hand Lord, while I run this race, 'cause I
Stand by me Lord, while I run this race, 'cause I

don't want to run this race in vain.
don't want to run this race in vain.
don't want to run this race in vain.

Setting: African-American spiritual, arr. Carl Harris, Jr. (b. 1935)

The eyes of all wait upon you

The eyes of all wait up-on you, O Lord and you give them their food in due sea-son. You o-pen wide your gra-cious hand and sat-is-fy the needs of ev-ery liv-ing crea-ture.

Words: Ps. 145:16-17 (BCP)
Music: *Bayou*, Carol Doran (b. 1936)
© 1996 Carol Doran

Glory to God

Glo-ry to God; Praise to the Son;
Glo-ry to God; Praise to the
Love to the Spi-rit; Three and yet One.
Son; Love to the Three and yet One.

Setting: John L. Bell and the Wild Goose Worship Group from *Come All You People*
© 1995 The Iona Community, admin. by GIA Publications, Inc.
You must contact GIA Publications, Inc. to reproduce this selection.

Through north and south

Through north and south and east and west May God's im-mor-tal name be blessed: Al-le-lu-ia, al-le-lu-ia! Till ev-'ry-where be-neath the sun, God's reign be-gins; God's will is done: Al-le-lu-ia, al-le-lu-ia, al-le-lu-ia, al-le-lu-ia, al-le-lu-ia!

Words: from *Songs of Praise*, alt.
Music: *Lasst uns erfreuen*, melody from *Auserlesene Catholische Geistliche Kirchengeseng*, 1623;
    Adapt. and harm. Ralph Vaughan Williams (1872-1958) alt.
© Oxford University Press

823

Benedictus benedicat

Be - ne - dic - tus be - ne di - cat, per Je - sum Chris - tum
De - o gra - tias, De - o gra - tias, per Je - sum Chris - tum

Dom - i - num no - strum. A - men.

Translation:

1. *May the Blessed One bless,*
   through Jesus Christ our Lord. Amen.

2. *Thanks be to God,*
   through Jesus Christ our Lord. Amen.

Setting: Miles Farrow

824

God grant them many years!

Spoken: To *(name)*, O Lord, grant long life and peace and protection and many years!

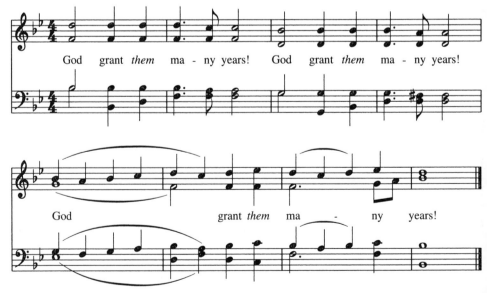

God grant *them* ma - ny years! God grant *them* ma - ny years!

God grant *them* ma - ny years!

Setting: Traditional Russian

Bless the Lord my soul

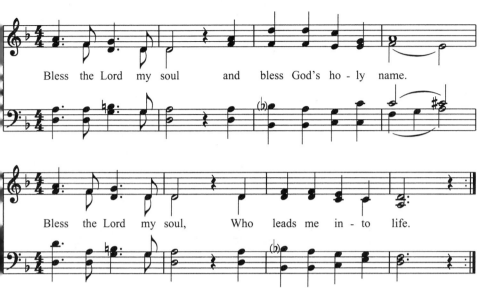

Bless the Lord my soul and bless God's ho-ly name.

Bless the Lord my soul, Who leads me in-to life.

Words: Psalm 103
Music: Jacques Berthier (1923-1994)
© 1984 Taizé, admin. GIA Publications, Inc.
You must contact GIA Publications, Inc. to reproduce this selection.

Stay with me

Noho pū

Stay with me, re-main here with me, watch and
No - ho pū, no - ho mai me ia'u, ki - a'i a

pray watch and pray.
pu - le, kiai a pule.

Words: Matthew 26, tr. Malcolm Naea Chun (b. 1954) © Malcolm Naea Chun
Music: Jacques Berthier (1923-1994)
© 1984 Taizé, admin. GIA Publications, Inc.
You must contact GIA Publications, Inc. to reproduce this selection.

O Lord hear my pray'r

O Lord hear my pray'r, O Lord hear my pray'r.

When I call, an - swer me. O Lord hear my pray'r. O

Lord hear my pray'r, Come and lis - ten to me. O

Words: Psalm 102
Music: Jacques Berthier (1923-1994)
© 1984 Taizé, admin. GIA Publications, Inc.
You must contact GIA Publications, Inc. to reproduce this selection.

828   Beati

Melody

Be - a - ti in do - mo Do - mi - ni Be -

Choral Accompaniment

Be - a - ti. Be - a -

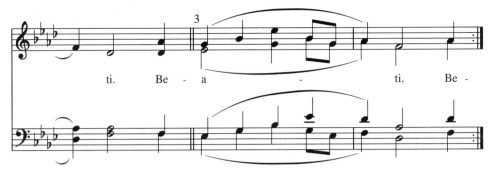

ti. Be - a - ti. Be -

Keyboard

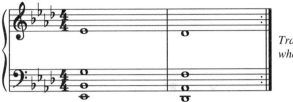

*Translation: Happy are they
who dwell in the house of God.*

Words: Matthew 5
Music: Jacques Berthier (1923-1994)

Laudate Dominum 829

Lau - da - te Do - mi - num, Lau - da - te Do - mi - num om - nes

gen - tes, Al - le - lu - ia. Al - le - lu - ia.

Translation: Praise the Lord, all you peoples.

Words: Psalm 117
Music: Jacques Berthier (1923-1994) © 1984 Taizé, admin. GIA Publications, Inc.

Laudate omnes gentes
E nā lāhuikanaka

Lau - da - te om-nes gen - tes, lau-da - te Do-mi - num. Lau -
E nā lā-hui-ka - na - ka ho - o - na-ni i ka Haku! E

Fine

da - te om-nes gen - tes, lau-da - te Do-mi - num! Lau -
nā lā-hui-ka - na - ka ho - o - na ni i ka Haku! E

Words: adapt. from the psalms, tr. Malcolm Naea Chun (b. 1954) © Malcolm Naea Chun
Music: Jacques Berthier (1923-1994) © 1984 Taizé, admin. GIA Publications, Inc.
You must contact GIA Publications, Inc. to reproduce this selection.

Ubi caritas
Aia nō e loaʻa

Descant

U - bi ca - ri - tas et a - mor
Ai - a nō e loaʻa ke a - lo - ha

A

U - bi ca - ri - tas et a - mor,
Ai - a nō e loaʻa ke a - lo - ha

u - bi ca - ri - tas, De - us i - bi est.
Ai - a nō e loa'a ke A - kua nō.

B

u - bi ca - ri - tas De - us i - bi est.
Ai - a nō e loa'a ke A - kua nō.

Translation: Where true charity and love abide, God is there.

Words: Latin, 8th c., tr. Malcolm Naea Chun (b. 1954) © Malcolm Naea Chun
Music: Jacques Berthier (1923-1994) © 1984 Taizé, admin. GIA Publications, Inc.
You must contact GIA Publications, Inc. to reproduce this selection.

Veni Sancte Spiritus   832

Ve - ni San - cte Spi - ri - tus.

Cantor

1. Come, Ho - ly Spir - it, from heav - en shine forth
with your glo - rious light. Ve - ni San - cte Spi - ri - tus.

2. Come from the four winds, O Spir - it, come breath of God; dis-
perse the shad - ows ov - er us, re - new and strength - en your

peo - ple. Ve - ni San - cte Spi - ri - tus.

Translation: Come, Holy Spirit.

Words: Pentecost Sequence; Taizé Community, 1978
Music: Jacques Berthier (1923-1994) © 1984 Taizé, admin. GIA Publications, Inc.
You must contact GIA Publications, Inc. to reproduce this selection.

833

The Lord's Prayer
(paraphrase)

Ostinato

Our Fa-ther in hea-ven, hal-low'd be your Name.

Cantor

Your king-dom come, your will be done, in earth as it is in

hea-ven. Give us to-day our dai-ly bread. And for-

give our sins as we for-give o-thers. Save us from the time of

tri-al, and de-li-ver us from e-vil. For yours is the

king-dom, the po-wer and the glo-ry are yours for e-ver. A-men.

Setting: Mark Peterson (b. 1952)
© 1995 Mark Peterson

Pater Noster

Our Father

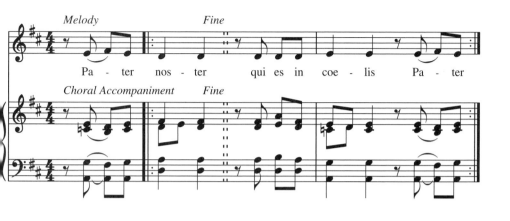

Melody — Fine

Pa - ter nos - ter qui es in coe - lis Pa - ter

Choral Accompaniment — Fine

Cantor (1) (2)

Pa - ter nos - ter qui es in coe - lis Pa - ter nos - ter qui es in

(3) *ad lib.* - - - - - - - - - - - - - - -

coe - lis Pa - ter nos - ter qui es in coe - lis qui es in

(4) ¬ (5)

coe - lis, qui es in coe - lis Pa - ter nos - ter qui es in

(6) (7)

coe - lis. A - men, a - men, a - men!

Setting: Jacques Berthier (1923-1994)

© 1984 Taizé, admin. GIA Publications, Inc.

You must contact GIA Publications, Inc. to reproduce this selection.

Service Music

Lord, have mercy

Kyrie

Lord, have mer - cy. Christ, have mer - cy. Lord, have mer - cy.

Setting: Don Pearson (b. 1959)
© 1995 Don Pearson

Lord, have mercy

Kyrie

Lord, have mer - cy. Lord, have mer - cy.

Setting: Peter Niedmann (b. 1960)
© 1996 Peter Niedmann

Kyrie eleison

Ky - ri - e e - lei - son.

Chris - te e - lei - son. Ky - ri - e e - lei - son.

Setting: Kevin R. Hackett (b. 1956), from *Hymn Tunes Mass*; based on *Herzliebster Jesu*, Johan Cruger (1598–1662), alt.
© 1991 CELEBRATION, Aliquippa, PA 15001. All rights reserved. International copyright secured. Used by permission.
You must contact CELEBRATION to reproduce this selection.

Lord, have mercy 838
Kyrie

Lord, have mer - cy.

Christ, have mer - cy. Lord, have mer - cy.

Setting: Kevin R. Hackett (b. 1956), from *Hymn Tunes Mass*; based on *Herzliebster Jesu*, Johan Cruger (1598–1662), alt.
© 1991 CELEBRATION, Aliquippa, PA 15001. All rights reserved. International copyright secured. Used by permission.
You must contact CELEBRATION to reproduce this selection.

Lord, have mercy
Kyrie

Lord, have mer - cy.

Lord, have mer - cy. Christ, have

mer - cy. Christ, have mer - cy.

Lord, have mer - cy.

(Ped.)

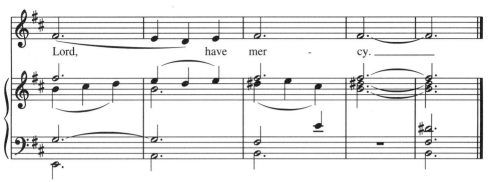

Lord, have mer - cy.

Setting: Arlen R. Clarke (b.1954)
© 1988 Arlen R. Clarke

Kyrie eleison

840

Leader

Ky - ri - e
Ky-ri - e e - le - i - son. Ky-ri-
e e - le - i - son. Christ - te e - le - i -
son. Christ - te e - le - i - son. Ky-ri-
e e - le - i - son. Ky-ri - e e - le - i - son.

Christ - te
Ky - ri - e

Setting: Betty Carr Pulkingham (b. 1928), from *Freedom Mass*, based on traditional African melodies.

841　　　　　　　　　　　　　　　　　**Kyrie eleison**

△ optional bells

Setting: Hildegard of Bingen (1098-1179);
tr. Lisa Neufeld Thomas (b.1947)

Lord, have mercy

Kyrie

842

△ Lord, have mer - cy. Lord, have mer - cy. Lord, have mer - cy. △

Christ, have mer - cy. Christ, have mer - cy. Christ, have mer - cy. △

Lord, have mer - cy. Lord, have mer - cy. Lord, have mer - cy. △

△ *optional bells*

Setting: Lisa Neufeld Thomas (b.1947)
from *Missa de Sancta Hildegard;*
melody adapt. from a Kyrie by Hildegard of Bingen
© 1996 Lisa Neufeld Thomas

Holy God

Trisagion

843

Ho - ly God, Ho - ly and might - y,

Ho - ly Im - mor - tal One, Have mer - cy up - on us.

Setting: John Karl Hirten (b.1956)
© 1995 John Karl Hirten

Holy God
Trisagion

Ho - ly God, Ho - ly and Might - y, Ho - ly Im -
mor - tal One, Have mer - cy up - on us. Ho - ly God,

1

Ho - ly and Might - y, Ho - ly Im - mor - tal One, Have

2

Ho - ly God, Ho - ly and Might - y,
mer - cy up - on us. Ho - ly God,
Ho - ly Im - mor - tal, One, Have mer - cy up - on us.

Ho - ly and Might - y, Ho - ly Im - mor - tal One, Have
Ho - ly God, Ho - ly and Might - y,

mer - cy up - on us, Have mer - cy up - on us.
Ho - ly Im - mor - tal One, Have mer - cy up - on us.

Setting: Mode 1 melody; Richard Fabian (b. 1942)
© 1984 All Saints' Company

Holy God

Trisagion

Ho - ly God, Ho - ly and Might - y, Ho - ly Im - mor - tal One,

Have mer - cy up - on us.

Setting: Carl Haywood (b. 1949), from *Mass for Grace*
© 1997 Carl Haywood

Holy God

Trisagion

Ho - ly, Ho - ly, Ho - ly God, Ho - ly God, Have

mer - cy on us. Ho - ly and Might - y and Might -

y, Have mer - cy on us. Ho - ly, Ho - ly, Im -

mor - tal One, Im - mor - tal One, Have mer - cy on us.

* May be sung as a round.

Setting: Ruth Boshkoff (b. 1934)
© 1996 Ruth Boshkoff

847

Alleluia with verses

Epiphany

Al - le - lu - ia, Al - le - lu - ia, Al - le - lu - ia, Al - le - lu - ia.

(Verse appointed for the day)

All repeat Antiphon

Setting: Tone 2; refrain from *Tibi, Christe, splendor Patris*, Moissac MS., 12th cent.;
 adapt. Marilyn L. Haskel (b. 1945)
 © 1997 The Church Pension Fund

848

Alleluia and verses

Eastertide

(Verse appointed for the day)

Setting: Tone 5, John L. Hooker (b. 1944);
 refrain after *Gelobt sei Gott*, Melchior Vulpius (1560?-1616)
 © 1996 John L. Hooker

The Nicene Creed
(Contemporary)

The congregation monotones on G throughout the Creed. Parts may be done by choir or organ.

We believe in one God, the Father, the Almighty,

maker of heav-en and earth, of all that is, seen and un-seen.

We believe in one Lord, Je-sus Christ, the on-ly Son of God,

eternally begotten of the Father, God from God, Light from Light,

true God from true God, be-got-ten, not made, of one Being with the Father.

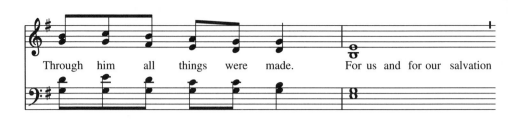

Through him all things were made. For us and for our salvation

he came down from heaven: by the power of the Holy Spirit

rit.

he became incarnate of the Vir - gin Mary, and was made man.

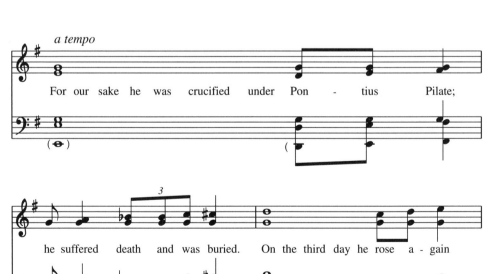

a tempo

For our sake he was crucified under Pon - tius Pilate;

he suffered death and was buried. On the third day he rose a - gain

* May be omitted

With the Father and the Son he is worshiped and glorified. He has spoken through the Proph - ets. We be - lieve in one holy catholic and apostolic Church. We ac - knowledge one baptism for the for-give-ness of sins. We look for the resur- rec - tion of the dead, and the life of the world to come. A - men.

Setting: Owen Burdick (b. 1954)
© 1985 Owen Burdick

Holy, holy, holy Lord

Sanctus

Ho - ly, ho - ly, ho - ly Lord, God of pow-er and might, __ hea - ven and earth are full of your glo - ry. Ho - san - na in the high - est. ___ * Bless - ed is he who comes in the name of the Lord. ___ Ho - san - na, Ho - san - na, Ho - san - na in the high - est, the high - est. ___

* optional text

Bless - ed is the one

Setting: Jonathan Dimmock (b. 1957), from *Missa Appalachia*
© 1996 Jonathan Dimmock

Holy, holy, holy Lord

Sanctus

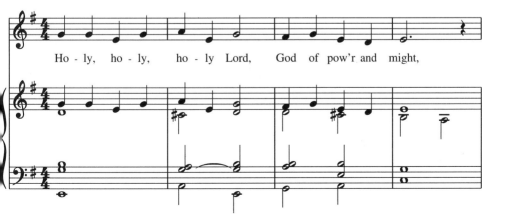

Ho - ly, ho - ly, ho - ly Lord, God of pow'r and might,

heav-en and earth are full of your glo-ry. Ho-san-na

in the high-est. Bless-ed is he who comes in the Name of the

Lord. Ho-san-na in the high-est.

Setting: Jack Warren Burnam (b. 1946)
© 1978 Jack Warren Burnam

852 **Holy, holy, holy Lord**
Sanctus

Ho-ly, ho-ly, ho-ly Lord,

God of pow-er and might. _____ Heav'n and

earth are full of your glo-ry. Ho-san-na in the

high - est. _____ Blessed is the one who comes in the

name of the Lord. Ho-san-na in the high - est. _____

Setting: William Bradley Roberts (b. 1947) from *Mass for St. Philip's*
© 1995 William Bradley Roberts

Holy, holy, holy Lord 853
Sanctus

Manual I

Ho - ly, ho - ly, ho - ly Lord,

Manual II

God of pow-er and might. Heav-en and earth are full of your glo-ry. Ho-san-na in the high-est.

Bless-ed is the one who comes in the name of the Lord.

Ho-san-na in the high-est.

Ho-san-na in the high-est.

Setting: John Karl Hirten (b. 1956)
© 1995 John Karl Hirten

Holy, holy, holy Lord

Santo

Ho-ly, ho-ly, ho-ly Lord, God of pow-er and might, heav-en and earth are full of your glo-ry. Ho-san-na. in the high-est. San - to, san - to, san - toes el Se -

Setting: Joel Martinson (b.1960), from *Missa Guadalupe*.

Holy, holy, holy Lord 855
Sanctus (Red Lake)

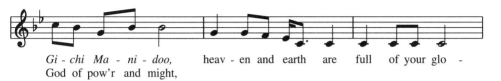

Ho - ly, ho - ly, ho - ly Lord, Ho - ly, ho - ly, ho - ly Lord,

Gi - chi Ma - ni - doo, heav - en and earth are full of your glo -
God of pow'r and might,

ry. Ho - san - na in the high - est.

Bless - ed is the one who comes in the name of the Lord. Ho -

san - na in the high - est.

Setting: Monte Mason (b.1949) after melodies found in *Chippewa Music* by Frances Densmore
© 1996 Monte Mason

Holy, holy, holy Lord 856
Sanctus

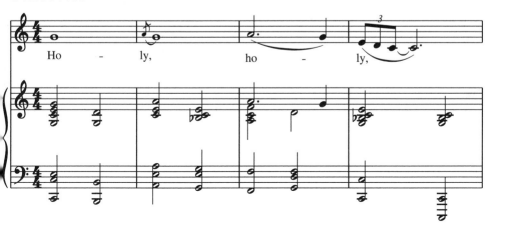

Ho - ly, ho - ly,

Music: Lena McLin, *Eucharist of the Soul*
Reprinted from *Eucharist of the Soul* (GC41)
© 1972 General Words and Music Co., San Diego, CA. Reprinted with permission 1997.

Holy, holy, holy Lord
Sanctus

857

Holy, holy, holy Lord
Sanctus

Ho - ly, ho - ly, ho - ly Lord, God of power and

might, heaven and earth are full of your glo - ry. Ho -

san - na in the high - est. *Bless - ed is he who comes

in the name of the Lord. Ho - san - na in the

high - est. Ho - san - na in the high - est.

* *Optional text:*

Bless - ed is the one

Setting: American folk melody; arr. Marcia Pruner;
    harm. Annabel Morris Buchanan (1889-1983)
    © Church Pension Fund

Holy, holy, holy Lord   859
Sanctus

Ho - ly, ho - ly, ho - ly Lord,

God of power and might,   hea - ven and earth are full of your glo - ry.

* *Optional choir part repeats first phrase here.*

Ho-san-na, Ho-san-na, Ho-san-na ___ in the high - est.

** Bless - ed is he who comes in the name of the Lord.

Ho-san-na, Ho-san-na, Ho-san-na ___ in the high - est.

** *Optional text:*

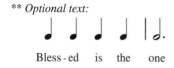

Bless - ed is the one

Setting: Ronald Arnatt (b. 1930) From WORSHIP II
Copyright © 1975, G.I.A. Publications, Inc.
You must contact GIA Publications, Inc. to reproduce this selection.

Memorial Acclamation
Prayer A

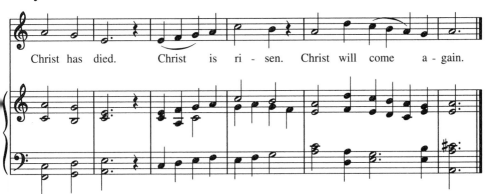

Christ has died. Christ is ri - sen. Christ will come a - gain.

Setting: Leonard Atherton (b.1941) from *Mass for Grace*
© 1997 Leonard Atherton

Memorial Acclamation
Prayer A

Christ has died. Christ is ri - sen. Christ will come a - gain.

Manual I

Manual II

(Pedal)

Setting: John Karl Hirten (b. 1956)
© 1995 John Karl Hirten

Great Amen

Manual I

A - men. A -

men. A - men.

Manual II

Great Amen

A - men. A - men. A - men.

A - men. A - men. A - men. A - men.

The Lord's Prayer
(Contemporary)

864

The Congregation may chant on a monotone G throughout. Parts may be done by choir or organ.

Setting: Owen Burdick (b. 1954)
© 1992 Owen Burdick

Fraction Anthem:
Christ our Passover

Al-le-lu-ia. Christ our Pass-o-ver is sac-ri-ficed for us; there-fore let us keep the feast. Al-le-lu-ia.

Setting: Thaddeus P. Cavuoti (b. 1955), from *Mass of St. Columba*
© 1995 Thaddeus P. Cavuoti

Fraction Anthem:
Christ our Passover

Cantor   Choir   Congregation & Choir

Al-le-lu-ia. Al-le-lu-ia. Al-le-lu-ia. Christ our Pass-o-ver is sac-ri-ficed for us; There-fore let us keep the feast. Al-le-lu-ia. Al-le-lu-ia. Al-le-lu-ia.

Setting: Owen Burdick (b. 1954)
© 1997 Trinity Episcopal Church

867

Fraction Anthem:
The bread which we break

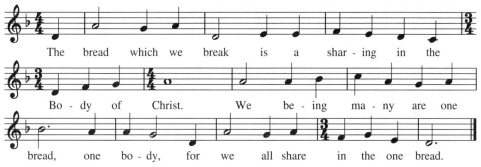

The bread which we break is a shar-ing in the Bo-dy of Christ. We be-ing ma-ny are one bread, one bo-dy, for we all share in the one bread.

Setting: Carl Haywood (b. 1949), from *Fraction Anthems, Canticles, and Chants*
© 1997 Carl Haywood

868

Fraction Anthem: Lamb of God
Agnus Dei

Lamb of God, you take a-way the sins of the world: have

Manual I

Manual II

mer-cy on us. Lamb of God, you take a-way the sins of the

Descant (Soprano/Tenor)

Lamb of God, you take a-

world: have mer-cy on us. Lamb of God, you take a-way the

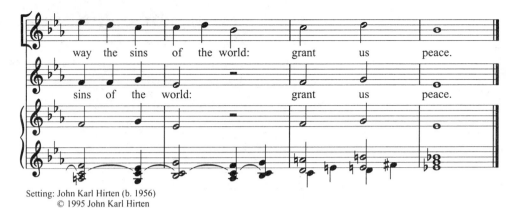

869   Fraction Anthem: Cordero de Dios
Lamb of God
Agnus Dei

ten pie-dad de no - so - tros, ten pie-dad de no - so - tros,

mi - se - re - re no - bis, mi - se - re - re no - bis,

1. 2.   **3.**

ten pie-dad de no - so - tros. Cor - da - nos, da - nos la paz.

mi - se - re - re no - bis. do - na no - bis pa - cem.

1. 2.   **3.**

Setting: Joel Martinson (b. 1960), from *Missa Guadalupe.*

Fraction Anthem: Cordero de Dios 870
Lamb of God
Agnus Dei

Cor - de - ro de Dios, tu que

qui - tas el pe - ca - do, del mun - do, ten pie -

dad de no - so - tros. Cor - de - ro de Dios, tu que

qui - tas el pe - ca - do, del mun - do, ten pie -

dad de no - so - tros. Cor - de - ro de Dios, tu que

qui-tas el pe-ca-do del mun - do. Da-nos la paz.

Fraction Anthem: Lamb of God   871
Agnus Dei

Lamb of God, you take a-way the sins of the world: have mer-cy on us. ___ Lamb of God, you take a-way the sins of the world: grant us peace.

872

Agnus Dei
Lamb of God

A - gnus De - i   qui   tol - lis   pec - ca - ta

mun - di,   Mi - se - re - re   no - bis.
(Do - na   no - bis   pa - cem).

*(To conclude, some sopranos and tenors of the choir
may sing the following several times as an ostinato.)*

Do - na   no - bis   pa - cem.

* *May be sung as a round.*

873

Fraction Anthem:
Those who eat my flesh

Al - le - lu - ia,   Al - le - lu - ia.   Those who

eat my flesh   and   drink my blood   a - bide   in me   and

Setting: Carl Haywood (b. 1949), from *Fraction Anthems, Canticles, and Chants*
© 1997 Carl Haywood

Whoever eats this bread 874

Principal Canon

Who - ev - er eats this bread will live for - ev - er.

Who - ev - er eats this bread will live for - ev - er.

Secondary Canons

A

This is the true bread which comes down from heaven, and gives life to the world.

B

Who - ev - er be - lieves in me shall not hun - ger or thirst, for the

bread which I give for the life of the world is my flesh.

Accompaniment

Words and Music: Eric H. F. Law (b. 1957) from *Christ, You Are In The World*
© 1986, 1992 Eric H. F. Law

Fraction Anthem:
Be known to us

Cantor or Choir

Be known to us, Lord Je - sus, in the
The dis - ci - ples knew the Lord Je - sus

1. *Congregation* 2. *Cantor or Choir*

break - ing of the bread. Be bread. The
The dis -

bread which we break, al - le - lu - ia, is the com -

Congregation

mun - ion of the bod - y of Christ. Be
The dis -

known to us, Lord Je - sus,
ci - pes knew the Lord Je - sus
in the break - ing of the

Cantor or Choir

bread. One bod - y are we, al - le - lu - ia, for though

man - y we share one bread. Be known to us, Lord
The dis - ci - ples knew the Lord

Congregation

Je - sus,
Je - sus
in the break - ing of the bread.

Setting: Gary James (b. 1957)

876

Fraction Anthem:
The disciples knew the Lord Jesus

Setting: Jack Warren Burnam (b. 1946)
© 1986 Jack Warren Burnam

Fraction Anthem:
The disciples knew the Lord Jesus

Cantor or Choir

The dis - ci - ples knew the Lord Je - sus in the break - ing of the

bread. *All* The dis - ci - ples knew the Lord Je - sus in the break-ing of the bread.

Cantor or Choir The bread which we break, al - le -

lu - ia, is the com - mun - ion of the bod - y of Christ. The dis -

ci - ples knew the Lord Je - sus in the break - ing of the bread. One

bo - dy are we, al - le - lu - ia, though ma - ny we share one bread. The dis -

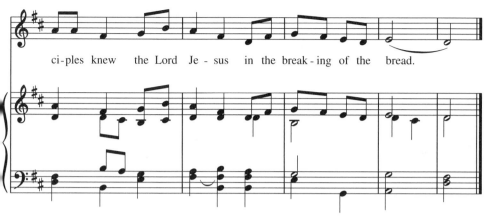

ci-ples knew the Lord Je - sus in the break-ing of the bread.

Fraction Anthem: 878
Whoever comes to me

Who - ev - er comes to me shall not hun - ger and

who-ev - er be - lieves in me shall nev - er thirst.

Christ our Passover

Pascha nostrum

Al - le - lu - ia

Cantor Alleluia

All Christ our Passover has been sacrificed for **us**;
    therefore let us keep the **feast**,
    Not with the old leaven, the leaven of malice and **e-vil**,
        but with the unleavened bread of sincerity and truth. Alle-**lu-ia**.

    Christ being raised from the dead will never die a**gain**;
        death no longer has dominion over **him**.
    The death that he died, he died to sin, once for **all**;
        but the life he lives, he lives to **God**.
† So also consider yourselves dead to **sin**,
        and alive to God in Jesus Christ our Lord. Alle-**lu-ia**.

    Christ has been raised from the **dead**,
        the first fruits of those who have fallen a**sleep**.
    For since by a man came **death**,
        by a man has come also the resurrection of the **dead**.
† For as in Adam all **die**,
        so also in Christ shall all be made alive. Alle-**lu-ia**.

Setting: Dorothy J. Papadakos (b. 1960)
© 1996 Dorothy J. Papadakos

Christ our Passover
Pascha nostrum

(metrical paraphrase)

Descant

3. In Christ we see the first fruits of the dead:

1. God's Pas - chal Lamb is sac - ri - ficed for us;
2. Now Christ is raised and will not die a - gain;
3. In Christ we see the first fruits of the dead:

though Ad - am's sin had doomed all flesh to die, in

There - fore with joy we keep the Eas - ter feast; for -
death has no more do - min - ion o - ver him; Through
though Ad - am's sin had doomed all flesh to die, in

Christ's new life shall all be made a - live. Al -

sak - ing sin, we share the bread of truth. Al -
him we die to sin and live to God. Al -
Christ's new life shall all be made a - live. Al -

le - lu - ia, Al - le - lu - ia!

le - lu - ia, Al - le - lu - ia!
le - lu - ia, Al - le - lu - ia!
le - lu - ia, Al - le - lu - ia!

The First Song of Isaiah

881

Ecce, Deus

Canticle 9

I will trust in the Lord, I will trust in the Lord, who's my sure de - fense and my friend.

Surely, it is God who **saves me;** *
    I will trust in him and not be a**fraid**
For the Lord is my stronghold and my sure de**fense,** *
    and he will be my **Savior.** *Refrain*

Therefore you shall draw water with re**joicing** *
    from the springs of sal**vation.**
And on that day you shall **say,** *
    Give thanks to the Lord and call upon his **Name**; *Refrain*

Make his deeds known among the **peoples;** *
    see that they remember that his Name is **exalted.**
Sing the praises of the Lord, for he has done great **things,** *
    and this is known in all the **world.** *Refrain*

Cry aloud, inhabitants of Zion, ring out your **joy,** *
    for the great one in the midst of you is the Holy One of **Israel.**
Glory to the Father, and to the Son, and to the Holy **Spirit:** *
    as it was in the beginning, is now, and will be for ever. **Amen.** *Refrain*

Setting: Music and refrain words by Carl Haywood (b. 1949),
    from *Fraction Anthems, Canticles, and Chants*
    © 1997 Carl Haywood

The First Song of Isaiah

Ecce, Deus

Canticle 9

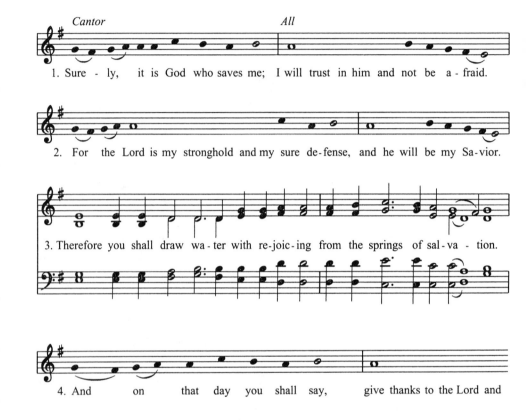

1. Sure - ly, it is God who saves me; I will trust in him and not be a - fraid.

2. For the Lord is my stronghold and my sure de - fense, and he will be my Sa - vior.

3. Therefore you shall draw wa - ter with re - joic - ing from the springs of sal - va - tion.

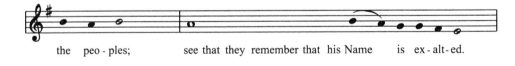

4. And on that day you shall say, give thanks to the Lord and

call up - on his Name; 5. Make his deeds known a - mong

the peo - ples; see that they remember that his Name is ex - alt - ed.

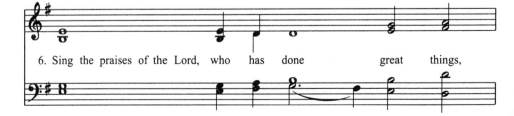

6. Sing the praises of the Lord, who has done great things,

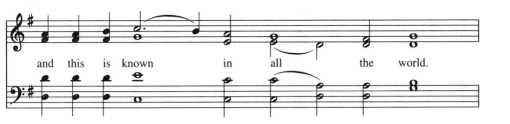

and this is known in all the world.

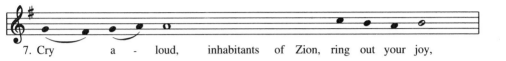

7. Cry a - loud, inhabitants of Zion, ring out your joy,

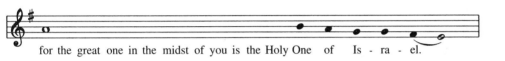

for the great one in the midst of you is the Holy One of Is - ra - el.

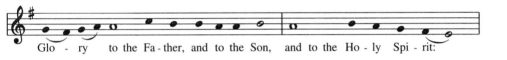

Glo - ry to the Fa - ther, and to the Son, and to the Ho - ly Spi - rit:

as it was in the beginning, is now, and will be

for - e - ver. A - men.

Setting: Tone 7, polyphony alternatim after Leonhard Schroeter (c.1532-c.1601)
  arr. Fred Goff (b. 1952)
  © 1984 All Saints' Company

The Third Song of Isaiah
Surge, illuminare

Refrain

A - rise, shine, for your light has come, his glo - ry is up - on you.

Arise, shine, for your light has **come,** *
    and the glory of the Lord has dawned upon you.
For behold, darkness covers the **land;** *
    deep gloom enshrouds the **peoples.** *Refrain*

But over you the Lord shall **rise,** *
    and his glory will appear up**on you.**
Nations will stream to your **light,** *
    and kings to the brightness of your **dawning.** *Refrain*

Your gates will always be **open;** *
    by day or night they will never be **shut.**
They will call you, The City of the **Lord,** *
    The Zion of the Holy One of **Israel.** *Refrain*

Violence will no more be heard in your **land,** *
    ruin or destruction within your **borders.**
You will call your walls, Sal**vation,** *
    and all your portals, **Praise,**

† The sun will no more be your light by **day;** *
    by night you will not need the brightness of the **moon.** *Refrain*

Setting: Music and refrain words by Carl Haywood (b. 1949),
    from *Fraction Anthems, Canticles, and Chants*
    © 1997 Carl Haywood

A Song of Creation

884

Benedicite, omnia opera Domini

Canticle 12 (metrical paraphrase)

1. O all ye works of God now come to thank him and a - dore; O an - gels sing and
2. O sun and moon and stars of heav'n your end - less praise out - pour; O chang - ing sea - sons,
3. O heat and cold, O night and day, O storms and thund - er's roar, O fields and for - ests,
4. O earth and sea, O all that live in wa - ter or on shore, O men and wo - men
5. O let his peo - ple bless the Lord like right - eous souls of yore; let those of ho - ly,

bless the Lord   and praise   him ev - er - more.
bless the Lord   and praise   him ev - er - more.
bless the Lord   and praise   him ev - er - more.
bless the Lord   and praise   him ev - er - more.
hum - ble heart   come praise   him ev - er - more.

ev - er - more.

Words: F. Bland Tucker (1895-1984) © Church Pension Fund
Music: *Rockville* Thaddeus P. Cavuoti (b. 1955)
© 1995 Thaddeus P. Cavuoti

A Song of Creation

885

Benedicite, omnia opera Domini

Canticle 12 (metrical paraphrase)

1. Let all cre - a - tion bless the Lord, till heav'n with praise is ring - ing.
2. All liv - ing things up - on the earth, green fer - tile hills and moun - tains,
3. O men and wo - men ev - ery-where, lift up a hymn of glo - ry;

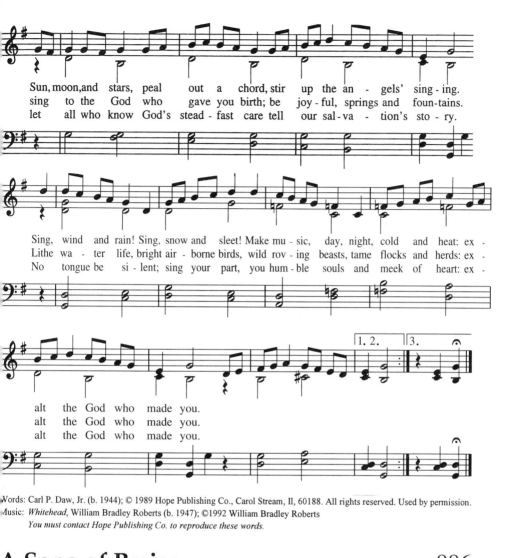

Sun, moon, and stars, peal out a chord, stir up the an - gels' sing - ing.
sing to the God who gave you birth; be joy - ful, springs and foun - tains.
let all who know God's stead - fast care tell our sal - va - tion's sto - ry.

Sing, wind and rain! Sing, snow and sleet! Make mu - sic, day, night, cold and heat: ex -
Lithe wa - ter life, bright air - borne birds, wild rov - ing beasts, tame flocks and herds: ex -
No tongue be si - lent; sing your part, you hum - ble souls and meek of heart: ex -

1. 2.   3.

alt the God who made you.
alt the God who made you.
alt the God who made you.

A Song of Praise

886

Benedictus es, Domine

Canticle 13

Glo - ry to you, O Lord,   glo - ry to you, O Lord,

you are wor-thy of praise.

Glory to you, Lord God of our **fathers**;*
   you are worthy of praise; glory to **you**.
Glory to you for the radiance of your holy **Name**;*
   we will praise you and highly exalt you for **ever**.   *Refrain*

Glory to you in the splendor of your **temple**;*
   on the throne of your majesty, glory to **you**.
Glory to you, seated between the **Cherubim**;*
   we will praise you and highly exalt you for **ever**.   *Refrain*

Glory to you, beholding the **depths**;*
   in the high vault of heaven, glory to **you**.
Glory to you, Father, Son, and Holy **Spirit**;*
   we will praise you and highly exalt you for **ever**.   *Refrain*

Setting: Music and refrain words by Carl Haywood (b. 1949),
   from *Fraction Anthems, Canticles, and Chants*
   © 1997 Carl Haywood

887   A Song of Praise
Benedictus es, Domine
Canticle 13

Glo-ry to you, Lord God of our fa-thers;   you are wor-thy of praise;

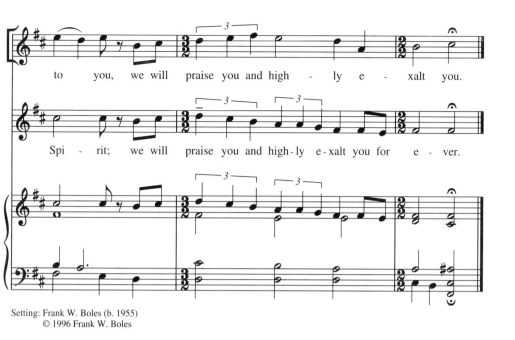

to you, we will praise you and high - ly e - xalt you.

Spi - rit; we will praise you and high-ly e-xalt you for e - ver.

Setting: Frank W. Boles (b. 1955)
© 1996 Frank W. Boles

A Song of Penitence 888
Kyrie Pantokrator
Canticle 14 (metrical paraphrase)

1. Al - might - y Lord Most High draw near whose awe - some
2. How mea - sure - less your mer - cies stand, the hope and
3. From such a heart we bend the knee and all our
4. So lift on high the Sav - ior's praise with all the

splen - dor none can bear; e - ter - nal God, in mer - cy hear,
pledge of sins for - giv'n; those sins, un - num-bered as the sand,
sin and shame con - fess. Lord, your un - worth - y serv - ants see,
hosts of heaven a - bove, and sing through ev - er - last - ing days

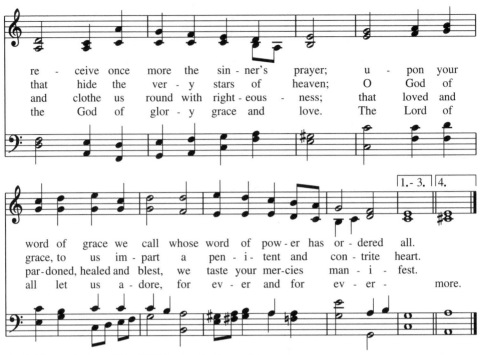

re - ceive once more the sin - ner's prayer; u - pon your
that hide the ver - y stars of heaven; O God of
and clothe us round with right - eous - ness; that loved and
the God of glor - y grace and love. The Lord of

[1.- 3.] [4.]

word of grace we call whose word of pow - er has or - dered all.
grace, to us im - part a pen - i - tent and con - trite heart.
par - doned, healed and blest, we taste your mer - cies man - i - fest.
all let us a - dore, for ev - er and for ev - er - more.

Words: Timothy Dudley-Smith (b. 1926), based on the *Prayer of Manasseh;*
© 1988 Hope Publishing Co., Carol Stream, IL 60188.
All rights reserved. Used by permission.
Music: *Keiser New*, Owen Burdick (b. 1954); © 1996 Owen Burdick.
You must contact Hope Publishing Co. to reproduce these words.

88.88.88

889   The Song of Zechariah
Benedictus Dominus Deus
Canticle 16 (metrical paraphrase)

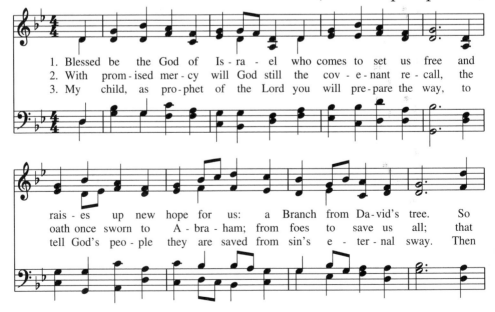

1. Blessed be the God of Is - ra - el who comes to set us free and
2. With prom - ised mer - cy will God still the cov - e - nant re - call, the
3. My child, as pro - phet of the Lord you will pre - pare the way, to

rais - es up new hope for us: a Branch from Da - vid's tree. So
oath once sworn to A - bra - ham; from foes to save us all; that
tell God's peo - ple they are saved from sin's e - ter - nal sway. Then

have   the   pro-phets long de - clared that with his might - y   arm   God
we   might wor-ship with - out fear   and   of - fer lives of   praise,   in
shall God's mer - cy   from   on   high shine forth and nev - er   cease,   to

would turn back our   en - e - mies and   all   that wish us   harm.
ho - li - ness and right - eous - ness to   serve God all   our   days.
drive a - way the   gloom of   death and lead us   in - to   peace.

Words: Carl P. Daw, Jr. (b. 1944) © 1989 Hope Publishing Co., Carol Stream,
        IL, 60188. All rights reserved. Used by permission.
Music: *Shepherd's Pipes* Annabeth McClelland Gay (b. 1925)
        © 1958 The Pilgrim Press, Cleveland, Ohio
        You must contact Hope Publishing Co. to reproduce these words.

                                                                    CMD

The Song of Zechariah   890
Benedictus Dominus Deus
Canticle 16 (paraphrase)

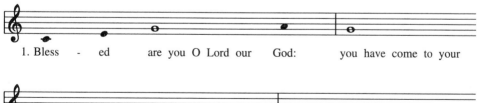

1. Bless - ed   are you O Lord our   God: you have come to your

peo - ple and   set them free.   2. You have raised up for us a mighty

Sa - vior: born of the house of your ser - vant Da - vid.

3. Through the voices of your ho - ly pro - phets, you have pro - mised since the world be-gan:

4. That you would save us from our e - ne - mies, and from the hand of all who hate us.

5. You pro - mised to show mercy to our fore - bears: and to remember your ho - ly co - ve - nant.

6. This was the oath sworn to our fa - ther Ab - ra - ham: that you would give us:

7. To set us free from the hands of our e - ne - mies, free to worship you with - out fear,

8. Ho - ly and righteous in your sight all the days of our life.

9. And you, child, shall be called the prophet of the Most High: for you will go before the face of the Lord to pre - pare the way

10. To give God's people knowledge of sal - va - tion: through the for - give - ness of their sins.

11. In the tender compassion of our God: the dawn from on high shall break up - on us,

12. To shine on those who dwell in darkness, and in the shad - ow of death: and to guide our feet in - to the way of peace.

Glo - ry to the Father, and to the Son, and to the Ho - ly Spi - rit; as it was in the beginning, is now, and e - ver shall be; through all ag - es. A - men.

Setting: Tone 5, Richard Fabian (b. 1942) Polyphony alternatim after Jacob Handl (1550-1591), adapt. from *Ecce quomodo moritur*
© 1972 All Saints' Company

The Song of Simeon

Nunc dimittis

Canticle 17 (paraphrase)

Refrain

Lord, you have ful - filled your word; now let your ser - vant de - part in peace.

Lord, you have ful - filled your word; now let your ser - vant de - part in peace.

1. 2. *Fine* (to verses)*

* *At end of canticle in Compline, repeat antiphon.*

1. With my own eyes I have seen the sal - va - tion, which

you have pre - pared in the sight of ev - 'ry peo - ple.

Refrain

Refrain

2. A light to re - veal you to the na - tions and the

glo - ry of your peo - ple Is - ra el.

Setting: *Port Arthur*, Mimi Fara (b. 1938); antiphon for use at Compline: Kevin Hackett (b. 1956)

Antiphon for use at Compline

Guide us wak - ing, O Lord, and guard us sleep - ing; that a -

wake we may watch with Christ, and a - sleep we may rest in

1. Before canticle

peace.

2. After canticle

peace.

Setting: Kevin Hackett (b.1956)

A Song to the Lamb

Dignus es

Canticle 18 (metrical paraphrase)

892

Descant (Soprano/Tenor)

3. To the Al - might - y, throned in heav'n - ly

1. Splen - dor and hon - or, ma - jes - ty and pow - er,
2. Praised be the true Lamb, slain for our re - demp - tion,
3. To the Al - might - y, throned in heav'n - ly splen - dor,

splen - dor, and to the Sav - ior, Christ our Lamb

are yours, O Lord God, fount of ev - ery bless - ing,
by whose self - off'r - ing we are made God's peo - ple:
and to the Sav - ior, Christ our Lamb and Shep - herd,

Shep - herd, praise, and glo - ry gi - ven,

for by your bid - ding was the whole cre - a - tion
a priest - ly king - dom, from all tongues and na - tions,
be a - dor - a - tion, praise, and glo - ry gi - ven,

now and for e -

called in - to be - ing.
called to God's ser - vice.
now and for e -

ver. Ah _____

ver. _____

Words: Carl P. Daw, Jr. (b. 1944)
  © 1990 Hope Publishing Co., Carol Stream, IL 60188. All rights reserved.
  Used by permission.
Music: Frank W. Boles (b.1955)
  © 1991 Frank W. Boles
  You must contact Hope Publishing Co. to reproduce these words.

A Song to the Lamb
Dignus es
Canticle 18

1. Splendor and honor and kingly power *royal* are yours by right, O Lord our God. *God Most High.*

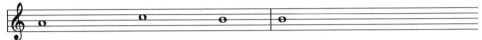

2. For you created everything that is, and by your will they were created and

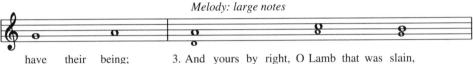

Melody: large notes

have their being; 3. And yours by right, O Lamb that was slain,

for with your blood you have re-deemed for God, 4. From every family, language,

people, and nation, a kingdom of priests to serve our God. *royal priesthood*

5. And so, to him who sits upon the throne, and to Christ the Lamb, *the One*

6. Be worship and praise, do-minion and splendor, for ever and for ever-more.

Setting: Richard Fabian (b. 1942)
© 1994 All Saints' Company

A Song to the Lamb

Dignus es

Canticle 18

Splen - dor and hon - or and roy - al pow'r are yours by right, O God Most High, For you cre - a - ted ev - ery - thing that

is,   and by your will   they were cre - a - ted and

have their be - ing; ___   And yours by   right, O Lamb that was

slain,   for with your blood,   you have re-deemed for God,   From

ev - ery fam - ily,   lan - guage, peo - ple,   and   na - tion,   a

Setting: James L. Denman (b.1952)
© 1990 James L. Denman

895

The Song of the Redeemed

Magna et mirabilia

Canticle 19

O ruler of the universe, Lord God
great deeds are they that you have **done**, *
   surpassing human under**standing**.
Your ways are ways of righteousness and **truth**, *
   O King of all the **ages**. *Refrain*

Who can fail to do you homage, Lord,
and sing the praises of your **Name**? *
   for you only are the holy **One**.
All nations will draw near and fall down be**fore you**, *
   because your just and holy works have been re**vealed**. *Refrain*

Glory to the Father, and to the **Son**,
and to the Holy **Spirit**; *
   as it was in the beginning, is **now**,
and will be for ever. **Amen**. *Refrain*

Setting: Music and refrain words by Carl Haywood (b. 1949),
  from *Fraction Anthems, Canticles, and Chants*
  © 1997 Carl Haywood

Gloria in excelsis

Canticle 20

Glo-ry to God in the high-est, and peace to his peo-ple on earth.

Manual I

Manual II

Lord God, heav'n-ly King, al - might-y God and Fa-ther, we

wor - ship you, we give you thanks, we praise you for your glo-ry.

Lord Je - sus Christ, on - ly Son of the Fa-ther,

Glory to God

897

Gloria in excelsis

Canticle 20

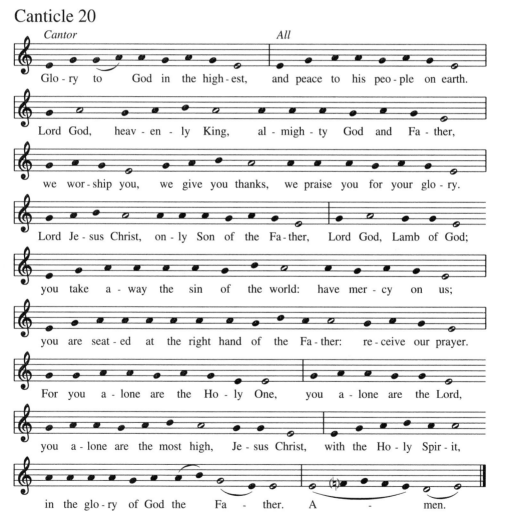

Glory to God
Gloria in excelsis
Canticle 20

Glory to God in the high-est, and peace to his peo-ple on earth.

Lord God, heavenly King, almighty God and Father, we worship you, we give

you thanks, we praise you for your glory. Lord Jesus Christ, only Son of the Father,

Lord God, Lamb of God, you take away the sin of the world:

have mer - cy on us; You are seated at the right hand of the Father:

re - ceive our prayer. For you alone are the Ho - ly One,

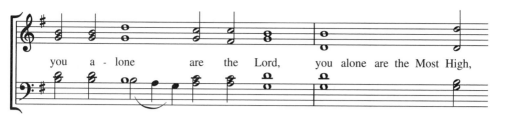

you a - lone are the Lord, you alone are the Most High,

Je - sus Christ, with the Ho - ly Spirit, in the glo - ry

of God the Fa - ther. A - men.

Setting: Fred Goff (b. 1952) after a melody att. Heinrich Isaac (1450? -1517)
Copyright © 1984 All Saints' Company

Glory to God 899
Gloria in excelsis
Canticle 20

Glo - ry,

wor-ship you, we give you thanks, we praise you for your glo-ry.

Lord Je-sus Christ, on-ly Son of the Fa - ther, Lord God, Lamb of

God, Glo-ry, Glo-ry, hal-le-lu - jah, Lord we praise your Ho-ly name, _

_ Glo-ry, Glo-ry ha-le-lu - jah, Lord we praise your Ho-ly name. _

You take a-way the sin of the world: have mer-cy on us; you are seat-ed at the right hand of the Fa-ther: re-ceive our prayer. For you a-lone are the

Descant: Lord, Lord _ hal - le - lu - jah.

Women: Glo - ry ha - le - lu - jah, Lord we Praise your Ho - ly

Men: Glo - ry ha - le - lu - jah, Lord we Praise your Ho - ly

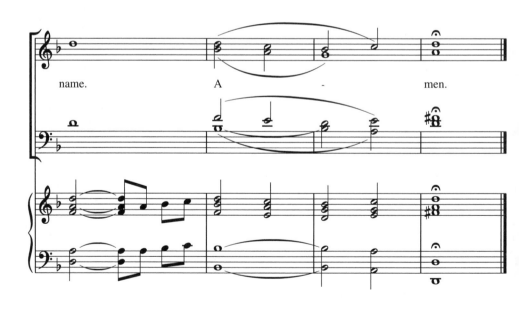

name. A - men.

Setting: Carl Haywood (b. 1949),
from *Mass for Grace,*
Copyright © 1992 Carl Haywood
You must contact Carl Haywood to reproduce this selection.

Glory to God

Gloria in excelsis

Canticle 20

Glo-ry to God in the high-est, ___ and peace to his peo-ple on earth. ___ Lord God,

(senza Ped. ad lib.)

heav'n-ly King, al-migh-ty God and Fa-ther, ___ we wor-ship

(Ped.)

Lord, _____ you a - lone are the Most High, Je - sus Christ, with the Ho - ly Spi - rit, _____ in the glo - ry of God the Fa - ther. A - men. _____

Setting: John Rutter (b. 1945)
Copyright © Oxford University Press

Glory to God

Gloria in excelsis

Canticle 20

re - ceive our prayer. For you a- lone are the Ho-ly One, you a - lone are the Lord, you a- lone are the Most High, Je-sus Christ, with the Ho-ly Spir-it, in the glo - ry of God the Fa - ther. A - men.

a tempo

Senza Ped. Ped.

Setting: Ronald Arnatt (b. 1930)

902

You are God
Te Deum laudamus
Canticle 21

1. You are God: we praise you; You are the Lord: we ac-claim you;

2. You are the eternal Fa-ther: All cre-a-tion wor-ships you.

3. To you all angels, all the pow'rs of hea-ven, Cherubim and Seraphim,

sing in end-less praise: 4. Holy, holy, holy Lord

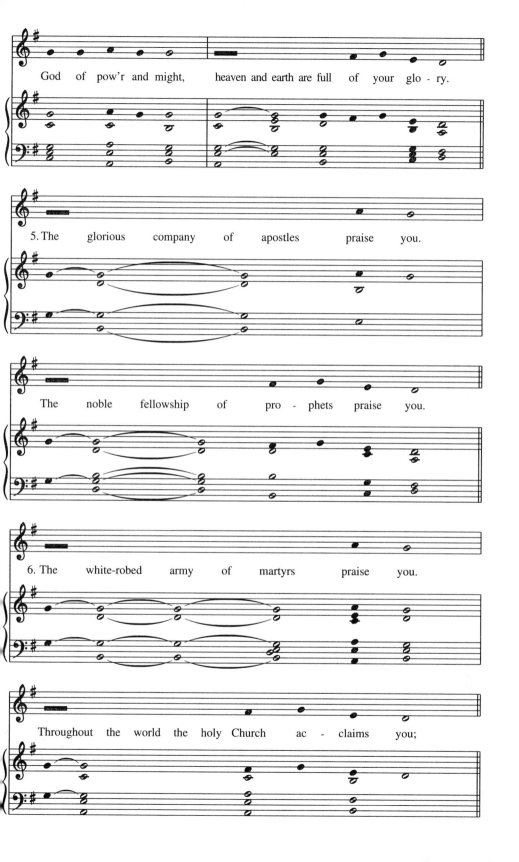

God of pow'r and might, heaven and earth are full of your glo-ry.

5. The glorious company of apostles praise you.

The noble fellowship of pro - phets praise you.

6. The white-robed army of martyrs praise you.

Throughout the world the holy Church ac - claims you;

7. Father, of majesty unbound - ed, your true and only Son.

worthy of all wor - ship, 8. and the Holy Spirit ad - vo - cate and guide.

9. You, Christ, are the king of glo - ry, the eternal Son of the Fa - ther.

10. When you became man to set us free you did not shun the Vir - gins' womb.

11. You overcame the sting of death and opened the kingdom of

heaven to all be - liev - ers. 12. You are seated at God's right hand in glo - ry.

We believe that you will come and be our judge.

13. Come then, Lord, and help your peo - ple, bought with the price of your own blood,

14. and bring us with your saints to glory ev - er - last - ing.

Setting: Plainsong, Tone 8; adapt. John L. Hooker (b. 1994)
Copyright © 1997 John L. Hooker

903

You are God
Te Deum laudamus
Canticle 21

1. You are ˈGod: we ˈpraise you; *
   You are the ˈLörd: ˈwe acˈclaim you;

2. You are the eˈternal ˈFather: *
   All creˈation ˈworships ˈyou.

3. To you all angels, all the ˈpowers of ˈheaven, *
   Cherubim and Seraphim, ˈsing in ˈendless ˈpraise:

4. Holy, holy, holy Lord, God of ˈpower and ˈmight, *
   heaven and ˈearth are ˈfull of your ˈglory.

5. The glorious company of aˈpostles ˈpraise you. *
   The noble ˈfellowship of ˈprophets ˈpraise you.

6. The white-robed army of ˈmartyrs ˈpraise you. *
   Throughout the world the ˈholy ˈChurch acˈclaims you;

7. Father, of ˈmajesty unˈbounded, *
   your true and only Son, ˈworthy ˈof all ˈworship,

8. And the ˈHoly ˈSpirit, *
   —ˈ advoˈcate and ˈguide.

9. You, Christ, are the ˈking of ˈglory, *
   the eˈternal ˈSon of the ˈFather.

10. When you became man to ˈset us ˈfree *
    you did not ˈshun the ˈVirgin's ˈwomb.

11. You overcame the ˈsting of ˈdeath *
    and opened the kingdom of ˈheaven to ˈall beˈlievers.

12. You are seated at God's right ˈhand in ˈglory. *
    We believe that you will ˈcome and ˈbe our ˈjudge.

13. Come then, Lord, and ˈhelp your ˈpeople, *
    bought with the ˈprice of ˈyour own ˈblood,

14. And bring us ˈwith your ˈsaints *
    to ˈglory ˈeverˈlasting.

Setting: Shirley Hill (b. 1933); after *Crucifer* by Sydney Hugo Nicholson (1875-1947)
Music ©1974 by Hope Publishing Co., Carol Stream, IL 60188. All rights reserved. Used by Permission.
You must contact Hope Publishing Co. to reproduce this music.

A Song of Wisdom

Sapientia liberavit

Canticle A

1. Wisdom freed from a nation of op-pressors a holy people and a blame-less race;

2. She entered the soul of a servant of the Lord, withstood dread rulers with won-ders and signs.

3. To the saints she gave the reward of their labors, and led them by a mar-velous way;

Manual only

4. She was their shelter by day and a blaze of stars by night.

5. She brought them across the Red Sea, she led them through might-y wa-ters;

6. But their enemies she swallowed in the waves and spewed them out from the

depths of the a-byss. 7. And then, Lord, the righteous sang hymns to your Name,

and praised with one voice your pro-tect-ing hand; 8. For Wisdom opened the

mouths of the mute, and gave speech to the tongues of a new-born people.

Ped.

Setting: Dent Davidson (b. 1960)

A Song of Wisdom

Sapientia liberavit

905

Canticle A (metrical paraphrase)

1. Wisdom freed a holy people, blameless from oppressors' sword,
2. Through the Red Sea safely brought them, led along the waters steep,

and withstood, with signs and wonders, rulers dread to serve the Lord.
but their enemies she swallowed, overwhelmed them in the deep.

Giving them reward of labors, led the saints along her way,
For salvation, Lord, the righteous praised your name with one accord:

she was blaze of stars in darkness and a shelter through the day.
song-filled tongues of new-born people uttered Wisdom's mighty word.

Words: Patricia B. Clark (b. 1938) © 1994 Patricia B. Clark
Music: *Brewer,* David Ashley White (b. 1944) © 1991 Selah Publishing Co., Inc.
You must contact Selah Publishing Co., Inc. To reproduce the music.

906

A Song of Pilgrimage
Priusquam errarem
Canticle B (metrical paraphrase)

1. Ev - en when young, I prayed for wis - dom's grace;
2. My foot has firm - ly walked the path of truth;
3. Glo - ry to one who gives me wis - dom's prize;
4. Some - thing with - in my be - ing has been stirred;

In tem - ple courts I sought her day and night, And I will seek her
With dil - i - gence, I fol - lowed her de - sign. My ear was o - pen
I vowed to live ac - cord - ing to her way. She gave me cour - age
My seek - ing brought a gift be - yond com - pare: The gift of lan - guage

to the ver - y end; she is my heart's de - light.
to re - ceive her words; Now wis - dom's skill is mine.
from the ve - ry start; She will not let me stray.
loosed my halt - ing tongue; God's praise is now my prayer.

Words: Patricia B. Clark (b. 1938)
    © 1995 Patricia B. Clark
Music: *Diligence*, Thomas Pavlechko (b. 1962)
    © 1996 Thomas Pavlechko

Indices

Copyrights

Acknowledgment

Every effort has been made to determine the owner and/or administrator of copyrighted material in this book and to obtain the necessary permission. After being given written notice, the publisher will make necessary correction(s) in subsequent printings.

Permission

The publisher gratefully acknowledges all copyright holders who have permitted the reproduction of their materials in this book. We especially thank those who have consented to allow Church Publishing to issue one-time, not-for-profit use free of charge. **You must contact Church Publishing in writing to obtain this permission.** (See address, phone, fax, and email below.) Certain selections will note those copyright holder(s) who require that you contact them directly to obtain permission to reprint their materials.

For extended or for-profit use of copyrighted materials in this book, you must write directly to the copyright holder(s). Contact Church Publishing for information. Phone: 1-800-223-6602 Fax: 1-212-779-3392 e-mail: copyrights@cpg.org   Address: 445 Fifth Avenue, New York, NY 10016

Abingdon Press
201 8th Ave., South
Nashville, TN   37203-0801
615-749-6158

AF-Foundation Hymns and Songs
Verbum
Mr. Hans Paulson
Box 15169
Stockholm, Sweden   10465
011-46-8-743-6500
Fax: 011-46-8-641-4585

All Saints' Company
c/o St. Gregory's Church
500 DeHaro
San Francisco, CA   94107

Boosey and Hawkes Inc.
35 East 21st Street
New York, NY   10010
212-358-5300
Fax: 212-358-5301
e-mail: bhsales@ny.boosey.com
www.ny.boosey.com

Celebration
PO Box 309
Aliquippa, PA 15001
724-375-1510
Fax: 724-375-1138
www.communityofcelebration.com

Chinese Hymnal Committee
China Christian Council
   The Rev. Cao Shenque
169 Yuan Ming Yaun Road 3/F
Shanghai   China   200002
86-21-63210806
Fax: 86-21-63232605

Church Pension Fund
Church Publishing Incorporated
445 Fifth Avenue
New York, NY 10016
800-223-6602
Fax: 212-779-3392
e-mail: churchpublishing@cpg.org

TCC- The Copyright Company
1025 16th Avenue South
Nashville, TN   37212
615-321-1096
Fax: 615-321-1099
e-mail: tcc@thecopyrightco.com

ECS Publishing
138 Ipswich Street
Boston, MA   02215-3534
617-236-1935
Fax   617-236-0261
www.ecspublishing.com

Faber Music Ltd.
(Contact Boosey and Hawkes Inc.)

General Words and Music Co.
(Contact Neil A. Kjos Music Co.)

GIA Publications, Inc.
7404 S. Mason Avenue
Chicago, IL   60638
800-442-1358
Fax: 708-496-2130
e-mail: custserv@giamusic.com
www.giamusic.com

Hal Leonard Publishing Corporation
7777 Bluemound Road
Milwaukee, WI   53213
414-774-3630
Fax: 414-774-3259
e-mail: halinfo@halleonard.com
www.halleonard.com

Harold Ober Associates, Inc.
425 Madison Avenue
New York, NY   10017
212-759-8600

Hope Publishing Co.
380 S. Main Place
Carol Stream, IL   60188
800-323-1049
Fax: 708-665-2252
e-mail: hope@hopepublishing.com
www.hopepublishing.com

JASRAC
3-6-12   Uehara
Shibuya-Ku
Tokyo 151, Japan
011-813-3481-2144
Fax: 011-813-3481-2153
www.jasrac.or.jp/ejhp

Lawson-Gould Music Pub., Inc.
c/o European American Music Distributors, LLC
PO Box 4340
15800 NW 48th Avenue
Miami, FL   33014
305-521-1604
Fax: 305-521-1638
www.eamdc.com

Lorenz   Corporation
501 East Third Street
P.O. Box 802
Dayton, Ohio 45402
800-444-1144
Fax: 937-223-2042
info@lorenz.com
www.lorenz.com

Manna Music Inc.
P.O. Box 218
Pacific City, OR   97135
503-965-6112
Fax: 503-965-6880

MorningStar Music Publishers, Inc.
1727 Larkin Williams Road
Fenton, MO   63026
800-647-2117
Fax: 314-647-2777

Neil A. Kjos Music Co.
4382 Jutland Drive
San Diego, CA   02117-3698
858-270-9800
Fax: 858-270-3507
www.kjos.com

New Dawn Music
(Contact   OCP   Publications)

New Zealand Prayer Book
The Anglican Church in Aotearoa,
     New Zealand and Polynesia
Mr. Robin Nairn
114 E. Queen Street
P.O. Box 885
Hastings, New Zealand
e-mail: gensec@hb.ang.org.nz

OCP   Publications
P.O. Box 18030
Portland, OR   97218-0030
800-548-8749
Fax: 503-282-3486
e-mail: liturgy@ocp.org
www.ocp.org

Oxford University Press
198 Madison Avenue
New York, NY   10016-4314
212-726-6000
Fax: 212-726-6444
e-mail: permissions@oup-usa.org

Paraclete Press
P.O. Box 1568
Orleans, MA   02653
800-451-5006

Pilgrim Press
700 Prospect Avenue East
Cleveland, OH   44115-1100
Fax: 216-736-3703

Plymouth Music Corporation
170 N. E. 33rd Street
P.O. Box 24330
Fort Lauderdale, FL 33307
954-563-1844

St. Vladimir Seminary Press
575 Scarsdale Road
Crestwood, NY 10707
914-961-8313

Selah Publishing Co., Inc.
P.O. Box 3037
Kingston, NY 12401
914-338-2816
Fax: 914-338-2991
selahpub@aol.com

Sisters of the Order of St. Benedict
104 Chapel Lane
St. Joseph, MN 56374-0277

Trinity Episcopal Church
Maria Campbell
74 Trinity Place
New York, NY 10006-2088
212-602-0800

Unichappell
(Contact Hal Leonard Publishing Corporation)

United Methodist Publishing House
(Contact Copyright Company)

Walton Music Corporation
(Contact Plymouth Music Corporation)

For all others please contact Church Publishing.

Authors, Composers, Arrangers, Translators, and Sources of Hymns and Spiritual Songs

Authors, Composers, Arrangers, Translators, and Sources of Service Music

Index of Scriptural References

Prayer of Azariah (NRSV)
Song of Three Young Men (RSV)

29-34	886, 887
32	745
35-65	884, 885

Prayer of Manasseh 888

Matthew

1:18-22	746, 747, 758, 807
2:1-12	726
2:2	847
4:4	847
4:23	847
4:24-25	774
5:3-12	828
5:14-16	775
5:38-42	792
6:9-14	864, 833, 834
8:1-4	734, 773
9:9-13	734
12:50	784
13:24-30	746, 747
14:22-33	800
16:24-26	734
17:5	847
18:19	807
21:9	850-859
21:15	850-859
21:8-9	728
21:12-17	746, 747
22:36-40	815
24:4-44	721
25:31-46	802
26:3-13	734
26:20	788
26:26-29	731
26:38b, 41a	826
27:27-45	735. 736
27:45	788
28:18-20	778, 780
28:19-20	848

Mark

1:15	847
1:16-21	757, 758, 807
1:40-45	734, 773
2:15-20	734
3:7-8	774
3:35	784
4:26-29	746, 747
5:19	847
8:34-9:1	734
11:8-10	728
11:15-19	746, 747
12:29-31	815
13:3-37	721

14:3-9	734
14:22-25	731, 732, 733
14:26	788
15:16-39	735, 736
15:34	788

Luke

1:68-79	888, 889,890
2:1-7	746, 747
2:14	848
2:1-18	724, 725, 726
2:29-32	891
2:41-52	746, 747
4:16-21	757, 782
4:18	847
5:1-11	757, 758, 807
5:12-16	734
5:27-32	734
6:17-19	774
6:20ff	811, 828
6:35	847
7:36-50	734
8:21	784
9:2	780
9:23-27	734
10:27	815
11:2-4	833, 834, 864
11:13	806
19:36-38	728
19:38	850-859
19:45-46	746, 747
21:25-30	721
22:14-20	731, 732, 733
22:40-46	826
23:19-20	780
23:24	780
23:26-49	735, 736
24:13-35	763, 799
24:32	848
24:35	875, 876, 877

John

1:1-18	748
1:11	788
1:14	782, 788
1:29	847
1:29, 36	868, 869, 870, 871, 872
2:11	847
2:13-25	746, 747
3:13-15	731, 732, 733
4:7-15	738, 784
5:7	740
6:25-62	760, 761, 762, 784
6:35b	878
6:33, 35, 51b,	874
6:55-56	873
6:68	847

Metrical Index of Tunes

The words in brackets are part of the first lines of hymns for which there are no tune names.

558. 558
[Baptized in water] 767

64. 64
Wildridge & St. Charles, Queensborough
    Terrace 750

65. 56
O-so-so 795

SM 66.86
Short Metre
Barnfield 798
Carlisle 771
Sterling 722
Shoshana 770
Sharpe 773

76. 76. D
Nyland 778
Redding 735

78. 78. D with Refrain
Nueva Creación 739

78. 98 with Refrain
[Shengye qing, Shengye jing] 725

75. 75. D
[Here, O Lord] 793

86. 85
Helensong 759

CM 86. 86
Common Metre
[A Song of Creation] 884
Dillow 807
Land of Rest 858

CMD 86. 86. D
Common Metre Double
Alexandra 788
Shepherd's Pipes 889

86. 86. 66. 86
[If you believe] 806

87. 87
Mariposa 726
Omni die 742
Peta 790

87. 87 with Refrain
Dominus regnavit 745

87.87. D
Arfon (Major) 769
Abbot's Leigh 780, 782
Domhnach Trionoide 768
Grid 753
Haywood's Home 754
Holy Manna 761
Raquel 763
Ton-y-Botel 721
Brewer 905

87. 87. 87
Monrovia 737
Sandria 746
Timeless Love 748
Urbs beata 747

87. 87. 887
Whitehead 885

87.98.87
Besançon Carol 724

LM 88. 88
Long Metre
Apple Tree 749
Berglund 765
Dunedin 779
Grace Church 731
Kedron 772
Lux vera lucis radium 732, 733
New Life 760
St. Martin 744
Tucker 774

LM with Refrain
88.88 with Refrain
Long Metre with Refrain
Sara H. 766

88.44.88 with alleluias
Lasst uns erfreuen

88. 88. 88
Owen 781
Keiser New 904

98. 89
Randolph 801

10 7. 10 7. 10 10 9. D
In dir ist Freude 738

10 10. 7
Piepkorn 777

10 10. 9 10
Peace 789

10 10 10 with Alleluias
Sine nomine 880, 775

10. 10. 10. 6
Diligence 906

10 10. 10 10
Ashley 741
Chappell 730
Dorland Mountain 799
Flentge 743
Sursum Corda 729
Woodslake 727

10 10. 10 10. 10 10
Song 1 776

10 10. 10 10 with Refrain
Hosanna 728

11 8.11 8. D
Samanthra 723

11 10. 11 10
Intercessor 734

11. 11. 11. 5
[A Song to the Lamb] 892

11. 11. 11. 10
Cantai ao Senhor 786

11 13. 11. 4
Song of Lau Tsu 803

12 11. 12 11. 11
El Camino 802

13 13. 7 7 13
Mary Alexandra 757

14 14. 14 14
Indifference 736

Irregular
[Ev'ry time I feel the Spirit] 751
Haleluya! Pelo tso rona 784
[It's me] 797
[I want Jesus] 805
Kusik 762
[Lead me, guide me] 756
Martin's Song 792
Pescador 758
[Peace before us] 791
[Precious Lord] 800
[Sweet, sweet Spirit] 752
[Santo] 785
Siyahamba 787
[Steal away] 804
[The steadfast love] 755
[Taste and see] 764
Thuma mina 808
Tjänsterna 794
Unidos 796
[Wade in the water] 740

Index of Tune Names

Index of First Lines

Italicized first lines are the second-language title.
Popular titles are in **bold**.

Service Music Index

First lines are in regular type.
Latin and Greek titles are in italics. Prayer Book and Hymnal titles are in bold.
Brackets indicate a paraphrase or variation on the authorized text.
Introductory antiphons to certain canticles are indicated by "(ant.)."